3rd Workshop on Computational Linguistics for Literature

(CLfL 2014)

AA005946

Held at the 14th Conference of the European Chapter of the Association for Computational Linguistics

Gothenburg, Sweden
27 April 2014

ISBN: 978-1-63266-404-4

Printed from e-media with permission by:

Curran Associates, Inc.
57 Morehouse Lane
Red Hook, NY 12571

Some format issues inherent in the e-media version may also appear in this print version.

Copyright© (2014) by the Association for Computational Linguistics
All rights reserved.

Printed by Curran Associates, Inc. (2014)

For permission requests, please contact the Association for Computational Linguistics at the address below.

Association for Computational Linguistics
209 N. Eighth Street
Stroudsburg, Pennsylvania 18360

Phone: 1-570-476-8006
Fax: 1-570-476-0860

acl@aclweb.org

Additional copies of this publication are available from:

Curran Associates, Inc.
57 Morehouse Lane
Red Hook, NY 12571 USA
Phone: 845-758-0400
Fax: 845-758-2634
Email: curran@proceedings.com
Web: www.proceedings.com

Preface

Welcome to the third edition of the workshop on Computational Linguistics for Literature. What started out two years ago as a small affair with an unorthodox title seems to be shaping into a modestly sized but vibrant research community.

Thanks to the effort of the authors and the program committee, April 27, 2014 promises to be an interesting day.

This year's workshop boasts the rich pickings of papers focussed on creating character representations from text and on applications of such representations. Agarwal et al. present a system for extracting social networks from movie scripts. Coll Ardanuy and Sporleder propose a method of finding similar novels using social networks as the underlying representation. Bullard and Alm work on identifying social information about characters from dialogues in a corpus of plays. Taking this a step further, Iosif and Mishra describe an integrated system for identifying and classifying characters in children's stories based on direct and indirect speech.

Taking a complementary point of view, the position paper by Levison and Lessard builds upon their previous work and proposes a graph-based representation for the temporal structure of narratives. The paper by Zemánek and Milička describes a diachronic study of Arabic literature, tracing the influence of certain treatises across centuries.

In the categories all of their own are two more papers. Davis and Mohammad break new ground with a paper on generating music from literature; you can listen to a one-minute musical summary of a novel. Mike Kestemont presents a position paper on authorship attribution, a topic which was quite popular in the 2012 and 2013 editions of the workshop.

Last but by no means least, we are delighted to have two invited speakers this year. An artist and researcher María Mencía from Kingston University in London will talk about electronic poetry. Jan Christoph Meister from University of Hamburg will tell us about the connections between narratology and computation.

We look forward to seeing you in Göteborg.

Anna Feldman, Anna Kazantseva, Stan Szpakowicz

Workshop organizers

Organizers:

Anna Feldman (Montclair State University)
Anna Kazantseva (University of Ottawa)
Stan Szpakowicz (University of Ottawa)

Program Committee:

Cecilia Ovesdotter Alm (Rochester Institute of Technology)
Apoorv Agarwal (Columbia University)
Julian Brooke (University of Toronto)
Hal Daumé III (University of Maryland)
David Elson (Google)
Micha Elsner (Ohio State University)
Mark Finlayson (MIT)
Pablo Gervás (Universidad Complutense de Madrid)
Roxana Girju (University of Illinois at Urbana-Champaign)
Catherine Havasi (MIT Media Lab)
Jerry Hobbs (University of Southern California)
Justine Kao (Stanford University)
Victor Kuperman (McMaster University)
Inderjeet Mani (Yahoo!)
Rada Mihalcea (University of Michigan)
David Mimno (Cornell University)
Saif Mohammad (National Research Council Canada)
Ekaterina Neklyudova (McMaster University)
Vivi Nastase (FBK Trento)
Owen Rambow (Columbia University)
Michaela Regneri (Saarland University)
Reid Swanson (University of California, Santa Cruz)
Rob Voigt (Stanford University)
Marilyn Walker (University of California, Santa Cruz)
Janice Wiebe (University of Pittsburgh)
Bei Yu (Syracuse University)

Table of contents

Workshop program

Sunday, April 27, 2014

	Session I
9:00–9:05	Welcome
9:05–10:00	*Language-Art Digital Poetics: An exploration of digital textualities in the production of artistic research* (invited talk) María Mencía
10:00–10:30	*Generating Music from Literature* Hannah Davis and Saif Mohammad
10:30–11:00	Coffee break
	Session II
11:00–11:30	*Computational analysis to explore authors' depiction of characters* Joseph Bullard and Cecilia Ovesdotter Alm
11:30–12:00	*Quotations, Relevance and Time Depth: Medieval Arabic Literature in Grids and Networks* Petr Zemánek and Jiří Milička
12:00–12:20	*Time after Time: Representing Time in Literary Texts* Michael Levison and Greg Lessard
12:20–12:30	Free-for-all
12:30–14:00	Lunch break

María Mencía is an artist-researcher and Senior Lecturer in New Media Theory and Digital Media Practice in the School of Performance and Screen Studies at Kingston University, UK. She holds a PhD in Digital Poetics and Digital Art by the University of the Arts, London. She studied English Philology at the Complutense University in Madrid, Fine Art and History and Theory of Art at the University of the Arts London.

Mencía's practice-based research in language, art and technology draws from different cultural, social, artistic and literary traditions such as: linguistics, fine art, film, visual, concrete and sound poetry, with digital poetics, electronic writing, and new media art theories and practices. Her practice includes interactive installations, performances, net.art, sound-generated poems and interactive generative narratives.

http://www.mariamencia.com/

Sunday, April 27, 2014 (continued)

Session III

14:00–15:00 *Between the Digital Scylla and the Hermeneutic Charybdis: Digital Humanities* (invited talk)
Jan Christoph Meister

15:00–15:30 *Structure-based Clustering of Novels*
Mariona Coll Ardanuy and Caroline Sporleder

15:30–16:00 Coffee break

Session IV

16:00–16:30 *From Speaker Identification to Affective Analysis: A Multi-Step System for Analyzing Children's Stories*
Elias Iosif and Taniya Mishra

16:30–17:00 *Parsing Screenplays for Extracting Social Networks from Movies*
Apoorv Agarwal, Sriramkumar Balasubramanian, Jiehan Zheng and Sarthak Dash

17:00–17:20 *Function Words in Authorship Attribution. From Black Magic to Theory?*
Mike Kestemont

17:20–17:30 Wrap-up

Jan Christoph Meister, a Professor of German Literature at the University of Hamburg, specializes in Narratology and Digital Humanities. He has published on narratological theory, humanities computing and various German authors, including Goethe, Gustav Meyrink and Leo Perutz. He currently serves as director of the Interdisciplinary Centre for Narratology at the University of Hamburg.

http://www.slm.uni-hamburg.de/ifg2/personal/jan-christoph-meister.html

Language-Art Digital Poetics: An exploration of digital textualities in the production of artistic research

María Mencía
Faculty of Arts and Social Sciences
Kingston University

Abstract

As an academic and an artist my practice-based research is at the intersection of language, art and digital technology. It explores the area of the in-between, the visual, the aural and the semantic. I am always interested in experimenting with the digital medium with the aim of engaging the reader/viewer/user in an experience of shifting 'in' and 'out' of language. This involves looking 'at' and looking 'through' transparent and abstract textualities and linguistic soundscapes. It draws from avant-garde poetics re-mediating concepts of reading and writing, exploring digital media grammars (voice activation, use of webcam, use of mouse, acts of revealing, triggering, cut and paste, dragging) for interactivity, aesthetics, engagement and meaning production. It is trans-disciplinary, bringing together different cultural, artistic and literary traditions such as: linguistics, fine art, visual, concrete and sound poetry, with digital poetics, electronic writing, and new media art theories and practices.

Between the Digital Scylla and the Hermeneutic Charybdis: Digital Humanities

Jan Christoph Meister
Department of Languages, Literatures and Media
Faculty of Arts
University of Hamburg

Abstract

The Digital Humanities are undoubtedly en vogue. Hardly any of the Humanities can nowadays ignore this methodological paradigm which affords us with vast resources of openly accessible digitized source material ranging from texts to multimedia files to 3D representations of material artifacts; with a plethora of digital research tools to explore and manipulate these primary resources; with virtual research environments that allow us to collaborate in real time across time and space; with exciting new forms of research publication and dissemination; and finally with big data approaches that have begun to balance the historically and qualitative oriented speculative concerns of the traditional Humanities with the more empirically oriented, descriptive research procedures of the Social Sciences.

To those who championed what was initially called 'Humanities Computing' since the late 1980s this development is of course rewarding. However, DH is not the first empiricist methodological paradigm whose advent the Humanities have witnessed during the latter part of the 20th century. Artificial Intelligence and Linguistics, to mention but two, also had their heyday – and in the 1970s many of us believed that these were to become the new master disciplines that would revolutionize the Humanities at large. It just didn't happen: Linguistics ranks as an equal again while AI has all but disappeared. DH, too, will experience its life cycle, and my personal prediction is that in ten years' time the term in its narrower sense of 'digital research methods in the humanities' will have become obsolete precisely because DH practices will by then have become business as usual for everyone.

Indeed, I think that there is something that is significantly more important than to engage in any such speculation about the future development of DH. One aspect that this methodological paradigm still lacks is a sufficiently developed critique of its own philosophical and epistemological fundamentals. If I were an opponent of DH this is the weak spot that I would attack relentlessly: how can a practice, a method, let alone a discipline that shies away from methodological self-reflection claim to be 'humanistic'?

Against this backdrop I would like to present some ideas on what I term the "DH-paradox": the inherent tension and, perhaps, even contradiction between the hermeneutic quest for holistic meaning (the German Sinn) - which, in Fregian terms, denotes more than just symbolic 'reference', but rather the coupling of reference and existential relevance that characterizes human symbolic systems and interactions – and the conceptual fundamental of the digital: the idea and premise that, whatever we want to study can be broken down into discrete, measurable atomic observations. The big and fascinating challenge for DH and for the Humanities, I believe, is how we can make this tension between the holistic and the atomic, the synthetic human experience and the analytic formalism of abstraction become productive from a Humanists perspective.

Generating Music from Literature

Hannah Davis
New York University
hannah.davis@nyu.edu

Saif M. Mohammad
National Research Council Canada
saif.mohammad@nrc-cnrc.gc.ca

Abstract

We present a system, *TransProse*, that automatically generates musical pieces from text. TransProse uses known relations between elements of music such as tempo and scale, and the emotions they evoke. Further, it uses a novel mechanism to determine sequences of notes that capture the emotional activity in text. The work has applications in information visualization, in creating audio-visual e-books, and in developing music apps.

1 Introduction

Music and literature have an intertwined past. It is believed that they originated together (Brown, 1970), but in time, the two have developed into separate art forms that continue to influence each other.[1] Music, just as prose, drama, and poetry, is often used to tell stories.[2] Opera and ballet tell stories through music and words, but even instrumental music, which is devoid of words, can have a powerful narrative form (Hatten, 1991). Mahler's and Beethoven's symphonies, for example, are regarded as particularly good examples of narrative and evocative music (Micznik, 2001).

In this paper, for the first time, we present a method to automatically generate music from literature. Specifically, we focus on novels and generate music that captures the change in the distribution of emotion words. We list below some of the benefits in pursuing this general line of research:

- Creating audio-visual e-books that generate music when certain pages are opened—music that accentuates the mood conveyed by the text in those pages.
- Mapping pieces of literature to musical pieces according to compatibility of the flow of emotions in text with the audio characteristics of the musical piece.
- Finding songs that capture the emotions in different parts of a novel. This could be useful, for example, to allow an app to find and play songs that are compatible with the mood of the chapter being read.
- Generating music for movie scripts.
- Appropriate music can add to good visualizations to communicate information effectively, quickly, and artfully.
  Example 1: A tweet stream that is accompanied by music that captures the aggregated sentiment towards an entity.
  Example 2: Displaying the world map where clicking on a particular region plays music that captures the emotions of the tweets emanating from there.

Given a novel (in an electronically readable form), our system, which we call *TransProse*, generates simple piano pieces whose notes are dependent on the emotion words in the text. The challenge in composing new music, just as in creating a new story, is the infinite number of choices and possibilities. We present a number of mapping rules to determine various elements of music, such as tempo, major/minor key, etc. according to the emotion word density in the text. We introduce a novel method to determine the sequence of notes (sequences of pitch and duration pairs) to be played as per the change in emotion word density in the text. We also list some guidelines we followed to make the sequence of notes sound like music as opposed to a cacophonous cascade of sounds.

Certainly, there is no one right way of capturing the emotions in text through music, and there is no one right way to produce good music. Generating

[1] The term *music* comes from *muses*—the nine Greek goddesses of inspiration for literature, science, and arts.

[2] Music is especially close to poetry as songs often tend to be poems set to music.

compelling music is an art, and TransProse can be improved in a number of ways (we list several advancements in the Future Work section). Our goal with this project is to present initial ideas in an area that has not been explored before.

This paper does not assume any prior knowledge of music theory. Section 2 presents all the terminology and ideas from music theory needed to understand this paper. We present related work in Section 3. Sections 4, 5, 6, and 7 describe our system. In Sections 8 and 9, we present an analysis of the music generated by our system for various popular novels. Finally in Section 10 we present limitations and future work.

2 Music

In physical terms, music is a series of possibly overlapping sounds, often intended to be pleasing to the listener. Sound is what our ears perceive when there is a mechanical oscillation of pressure in some medium such as air or water. Thus, different sounds are associated with different frequencies. In music, a particular frequency is referred to as *pitch*. A *note* has two aspects: pitch and relative duration.[3] Examples of relative duration are *whole-note*, *half-note*, *quarter-note*, etc. Each successive element in this list is of half the duration as the preceding element. Consider the example notes: 400Hz–quarter-note and 760Hz–whole-note. The first note is the sound corresponding to 400Hz, whereas the second note is the sound corresponding to 760Hz. Also, the first note is to be played for one fourth the duration the second note is played. It is worth repeating at this point that *note* and *whole-note* do not refer to the same concept—the former is a combination of pitch and relative duration, whereas whole-note (and others such as quarter-note and half-note) are used to specify the relative duration of a note. Notes are defined in terms of *relative* duration to allow for the same melody to be played quickly or slowly.

A series of notes can be grouped into a *measure* (also called *bar*). *Melody* (also called *tune*) is a sequence of measures (and therefore a sequence of notes) that creates the musical piece itself. For example, a melody could be defined as 620Hz–half-note, 1200Hz-whole-note, 840Hz-half-note, 660Hz–quarter-note, and so on. There can be one melody (for example, in the song *Mary Had A Little Lamb*) or multiple melodies; they can last throughout the piece or appear in specific sections. A challenge for TransProse is to generate appropriate sequences of notes, given the infinite possibilities of pitch, duration, and order of the notes.

Tempo is the speed at which the piece should be played. It is usually indicated by the number of beats per minute. A beat is a basic unit of time. A quarter-note is often used as one beat. In which case, the tempo can be understood simply as the number of quarter-notes per minute. Consider an example. Let's assume it is decided that the example melody specified in the earlier paragraph is to be played at a tempo of 120 quarter-notes per minute. The total number of quarter-notes in the initial sequence (620Hz–half-note, 1200Hz–whole-note, 840Hz–half-note, and 660Hz–quarter-note) is $2 + 4 + 2 + 1 = 9$. Thus the initial sequence must be played in $9/120$ minutes, or 4.5 seconds.

The *time signature* of a piece indicates two things: a) how many beats are in a measure, and b) which note duration represents one beat. It is written as one number stacked on another number. The upper number is the number of beats per measure, and the lower number is the note duration that represents one beat. For example, a time signature of $\substack{6\\8}$ would mean there are six beats per measure, and an eighth note represents one beat. One of the most common time signatures is $\substack{4\\4}$, and it is referred to as *common time*.

Sounds associated with frequencies that are multiples or factors of one another (for example, 440Hz, 880Hz, 1760Hz, etc) are perceived by the human ear as being consonant and pleasing. This is because the pressure waves associated with these sounds have overlapping peaks and troughs. Sets of such frequencies or pitches form pitch classes. The intervals between successive pitches in a pitch class are called *octaves*. On a modern 88-key piano, the keys are laid out in increasing order of pitch. Every successive 12 keys pertain to an octave. (Thus there are keys pertaining to 7 octaves and four additional keys pertaining to the eighth octave.) Further, each of the 12 keys split the octave such that the difference in frequency between successive keys in an octave is the same. Thus the corresponding keys in each octave form a pitch class. For example, the keys at posi-

[3]Confusingly, *note* is also commonly used to refer to *pitch* alone. To avoid misunderstanding, we will not use *note* in that sense in this paper. However, some statements, such as *play that pitch* may seem odd to those familiar with music, who may be more used to *play that note*.

tion 1, 13, 25, 37, and so on, form a pitch class. Similarly keys at position 2, 14, 26, 38, and so on, form another pitch class. The pitch classes on a piano are given names C, C#, D, D#, E, F, F#, G, G#, A, A#, B. (The # is pronounced *sharp*). The same names can also be used to refer to a particular key in an octave. (In an octave, there exists only one C, only one D#, and so on.) The octaves are often referred to by a number. On a standard piano, the octaves in increasing order are 0, 1, 2, and so on. C2 refers to the key in octave 2 that is in the pitch class C.[4]

The difference in frequency between successive piano keys is called a *semitone* or *Half-Tone* (*Half* for short). The interval between two keys separated by exactly one key is called *Whole-Tone* (*Whole* for short). Thus, the interval between C and C# is half, whereas the interval between C and D is whole. A *scale* is any sequence of pitches ordered by frequency. A *major scale* is a sequence of pitches obtained by applying the ascending pattern: Whole–Whole–Half–Whole–Whole–Whole–Half. For example, if one starts with C, then the corresponding C major scale consists of C, D (frequency of C + Whole interval), E (frequency of D + Whole interval), F (frequency of E + Half interval), G, A, B, C. Major scales can begin with any pitch (not just C), and that pitch is called the *base pitch*. A *major key* is the set of pitches corresponding to the major scale. Playing in the key of C major means that one is primarily playing the keys (pitches) from the corresponding scale, C major scale (although not necessarily in a particular order).

Minor scales are series of pitches obtained by applying the ascending pattern: Whole-Half–Whole–Whole–Half–Whole–Whole. Thus, C minor is C, D, D#, F, G, G#, A#, C. A *minor key* is the set of pitches corresponding to the minor scale. Playing in major keys generally creates lighter sounding pieces, whereas playing in minor keys creates darker sounding pieces.

Consonance is how pleasant or stable one perceives two pitches played simultaneously (or one after the other). There are many theories on what makes two pitches consonant, some of which are culturally dependent. The most common notion (attributed to Pythagoras) is that the simpler the ratio between the two frequencies, the more consonant they are (Roederer, 2008; Tenney, 1988).

Given a particular scale, some have argued that the order of the pitches in decreasing consonance is as follows: 1st, 5th, 3rd, 6th, 2nd, 4th, and 7th (Perricone, 2000). Thus for the C major—C (the base pitch, or 1st), D (2nd) , E (3rd), F (4th), G (5th) , A (6th) , B (7th)—the order of the pitches in decreasing consonance is—C, G, E, A, D, F, B. Similarly, for C minor—C (the base pitch, or 1st), D (2nd), D# (3rd), F (4th), G (5th), G# (6th), A# (7th)—the order of pitches in decreasing consonance is—C, G, D#, G#, D, F, A#. We will use these orders in TransProse to generate more discordant and unstable pitches to reflect higher emotion word densities in the novels.

3 Related Work

This work is related to automatic sentiment and emotion analysis of text (computational linguistics), the generation of music (music theory), as well as the perception of music (psychology).

Sentiment analysis techniques aim to determine the evaluative nature of text—*positive, negative,* or *neutral.* They have been applied to many different kinds of texts including customer reviews (Pang and Lee, 2008), newspaper headlines (Bellegarda, 2010), emails (Liu et al., 2003; Mohammad and Yang, 2011), blogs (Genereux and Evans, 2006; Mihalcea and Liu, 2006), and tweets (Pak and Paroubek, 2010; Agarwal et al., 2011; Thelwall et al., 2011; Brody and Diakopoulos, 2011; Aisopos et al., 2012; Bakliwal et al., 2012). Surveys by Pang and Lee (2008) and Liu and Zhang (2012) give a summary of many of these approaches. Emotion analysis and affective computing involve the detection of emotions such as *joy, anger, sadness,* and *anticipation* in text. A number of approaches for emotion analysis have been proposed in recent years (Boucouvalas, 2002; Zhe and Boucouvalas, 2002; Aman and Szpakowicz, 2007; Neviarouskaya et al., 2009; Kim et al., 2009; Bollen et al., 2009; Tumasjan et al., 2010). Text-to-speech synthesis employs emotion detection to produce speech consistent with the emotions in the text (Iida et al., 2000; Pierre-Yves, 2003; Schröder, 2009). See surveys by Picard (2000) and Tao and Tan (2005) for a broader review of the research in this area.

[4]The frequencies of piano keys at a given position across octaves is in log scale. For example, frequencies of C1, C2,..., and so on are in log scale. The perception of sound (frequency) in the human ear is also roughly logarithmic. Also, the frequency 440Hz (mentioned above) is A4 and it is the customary tuning standard for musical pitch.

Some prior empirical sentiment analysis work focuses specifically on literary texts. Alm and Sproat (2005) analyzed twenty two Brothers Grimm fairy tales to show that fairy tales often began with a neutral sentence and ended with a happy sentence. Mohammad (2012) visualized the emotion word densities in novels and fairy tales. Volkova et al. (2010) study human annotation of emotions in fairy tales. However, there exists no work connecting automatic detection of sentiment with the automatic generation of music.

Methods for both sentiment and emotion analysis often rely on lexicons of words associated with various affect categories such as positive and negative sentiment, and emotions such as joy, sadness, fear, and anger. The WordNet Affect Lexicon (WAL) (Strapparava and Valitutti, 2004) has a few hundred words annotated with associations to a number of affect categories including the six Ekman emotions (joy, sadness, anger, fear, disgust, and surprise).[5] The NRC Emotion Lexicon, compiled by Mohammad and Turney (2010; 2013), has annotations for about 14000 words with eight emotions (six of Ekman, trust, and anticipation).[6] We use this lexicon in our project.

Automatic or semi-automatic generation of music through computer algorithms was first popularized by Brian Eno (who coined the term *generative music*) and David Cope (Cope, 1996). Lerdahl and Jackendoff (1983) authored a seminal book on the generative theory of music. Their work greatly influenced future work in automatic generation of music such as that of Collins (2008) and Biles (1994). However, these pieces did not attempt to explicitly capture emotions.

Dowling and Harwood (1986) showed that vast amounts of information are processed when listening to music, and that the most expressive quality that one perceives is emotion. The communication of emotions in non-verbal utterances and in music show how emotions in music have an evolutionary basis (Rousseau, 2009; Spencer, 1857; Juslin and Laukka, 2003). There are many known associations between music and emotions:

- *Loudness*: Loud music is associated with intensity, power, and anger, whereas soft music is associated with sadness or fear (Gabrielsson and Lindström, 2001).
- *Melody*: A sequence of consonant notes is associated with joy and calm, whereas a sequence of disconsonant notes is associated with excitement, anger, or unpleasantness (Gabrielsson and Lindström, 2001).
- *Major and Minor Keys*: Major keys are associated with happiness, whereas minor keys are associated with sadness (Hunter et al., 2010; Hunter et al., 2008; Ali and Peynirciolu, 2010; Gabrielsson and Lindström, 2001; Webster and Weir, 2005).
- *Tempo*: Fast tempo is associated with happiness or excitement (Hunter et al., 2010; Hunter et al., 2008; Ali and Peynirciolu, 2010; Gabrielsson and Lindström, 2001; Webster and Weir, 2005).

Studies have shown that even though many of the associations mentioned above are largely universal, one's own culture also influences the perception of music (Morrison and Demorest, 2009; Balkwill and Thompson, 1999).

4 Our System: TransProse

Our system, which we call TransProse, generates music according to the use of emotion words in a given novel. It does so in three steps: First, it analyzes the input text and generates an emotion profile. The emotion profile is simply a collection of various statistics about the presence of emotion words in the text. Second, based on the emotion profile of the text, the system generates values for tempo, scale, octave, notes, and the sequence of notes for multiple melodies. Finally, these values are provided to JFugue, an open-source Java API for programming music, that generates the appropriate audio file. In the sections ahead, we describe the three steps in more detail.

5 Calculating Emotion Word Densities

Given a novel in electronic form, we use the NRC Emotion Lexicon (Mohammad and Turney, 2010; Mohammad and Turney, 2013) to identify the number of words in each chapter that are associated with an affect category. We generate counts for eight emotions (anticipation, anger, joy, fear, disgust, sadness, surprise, and trust) as well as for positive and negative sentiment. We partition the novel into four sections representing the beginning, early middle, late middle, and end. Each section is further partitioned into four sub-sections.

[5] `http://wndomains.fbk.eu/wnaffect.html`

[6] `http://www.purl.org/net/NRCemotionlexicon`

The number of sections, the number of subsections per section, and the number of notes generated for each of the subsections together determine the total number of notes generated for the novel. Even though we set the number of sections and number of sub-sections to four each, these settings can be varied, especially for significantly longer or shorter pieces of text.

For each section and for each sub-section the ratio of emotion words to the total number of words is calculated. We will refer to this ratio as the *overall emotions density*. We also calculate densities of particular emotions, for example, the *joy density*, *anger density*, etc. As described in the section ahead, the emotion densities are used to generate sequences of notes for each of the subsections.

6 Generating Music Specifications

Each of the pieces presented in this paper are for the piano with three simultaneous, but different, melodies coming together to form the musical piece. Two melodies sounded too thin (simple), and four or more melodies sounded less cohesive.

6.1 Major and Minor Keys

Major keys generally create a more positive atmosphere in musical pieces, whereas minor keys tend to produce pieces with more negative undertones (Hunter et al., 2010; Hunter et al., 2008; Ali and Peynirciolu, 2010; Gabrielsson and Lindström, 2001; Webster and Weir, 2005). No consensus has been reached on whether particular keys themselves (for example, A minor vs E minor) evoke different emotions, and if so, what emotions are evoked by which keys. For this reason, the prototype of Transprose does not consider different keys; the chosen key for the produced musical pieces is limited to either C major or C minor. (C major was chosen because it is a popular choice when teaching people music. It is simple because it does not have any sharps. C minor was chosen as it is the minor counterpart of C major.)

Whether the piece is major or minor is determined by the ratio of the number of positive words to the number of negative words in the entire novel. If the ratio is higher than 1, C major is used, that is, only pitches pertaining to C major are played. If the ratio is 1 or lower, C minor is used.

Experimenting with keys other than C major and C minor is of interest for future work. Furthermore, the eventual intent is to include mid-piece key changes for added effect. For example, changing the key from C major to A minor when the plot suddenly turns sad. The process of changing key is called modulation. Certain transitions such as moving from C major to A minor are commonly used and musically interesting.

6.2 Melodies

We use three melodies to capture the change in emotion word usage in the text. The notes in one melody are based on the overall emotion word density (the emotion words associated with any of the eight emotions in the NRC Emotion Lexicon). We will refer to this melody, which is intended to capture the overarching emotional movement, as *melody o* or M_o (the 'o' stands for overall emotion). The notes in the two other melodies, *melody e1* (M_{e1}) and *melody e2* (M_{e2}), are determined by the most prevalent and second most prevalent emotions in the text, respectively. Precisely how the notes are determined is described in the next sub-section, but first we describe how the octaves of the notes is determined.

The octave of melody o is proportional to the difference between the joy and sadness densities of the novel. We will refer to this difference by *JS*. We calculated the lowest density difference (JS_{min}) and highest JS score (JS_{max}) in a collection of novels. For a novel with density difference, *JS*, the score is linearly mapped to octave 4, 5, or 6 of a standard piano, as per the formula shown below:

$$Oct(M_o) = 4 + r\left(\frac{(JS - JS_{min}) * (6 - 4)}{JS_{max} - JS_{min}}\right) \quad (1)$$

The function r rounds the expression to the closest integer. Thus scores closer to JS_{min} are mapped to octave 4, scores closer to JS_{max} are mapped to octave 6, and those in the middle are mapped to octave 5.

The octave of M_{e1} is calculated as follows:

$$Oct(M_{e1}) = \begin{cases} Oct(M_o) + 1, & \text{if } e1 \text{ is joy or trust} \\ Oct(M_o) - 1, & \text{if } e1 \text{ is anger, fear,} \\ & \text{sadness, or disgust} \\ Oct(M_o), & \text{otherwise} \end{cases} \quad (2)$$

That is, M_{e1} is set to:

- an octave higher than the octave of M_o if e_1 is a positive emotion,

- an octave lower than the octave of M_o if e_1 is a negative emotion,
- the same octave as that of M_o if e_1 is surprise or anticipation.

Recall that higher octaves evoke a sense of positivity, whereas lower octaves evoke a sense of negativity. The octave of M_{e2} is calculated exactly as that of M_{e1}, except that it is based on the second most prevalent emotion (and not the most prevalent emotion) in the text.

6.3 Structure and Notes

As mentioned earlier, TransProse generates three melodies that together make the musical piece for a novel. The method for generating each melody is the same, with the exception that the three melodies (M_o, M_{e1}, and M_{e2}) are based on the overall emotion density, predominant emotion's density, and second most dominant emotion's density, respectively. We describe below the method common for each melody, and use *emotion word density* as a stand in for the appropriate density.

Each melody is made up of four sections, representing four sections of the novel (the beginning, early middle, late middle, and end).In turn, each section is represented by four measures. Thus each measure corresponds to a quarter of a section (a sub-section). A measure, as defined earlier, is a series of notes. The number of notes, the pitch of each note, and the relative duration of each note are determined such that they reflect the emotion word densities in the corresponding part of the novel.

Number of Notes: In our implementation, we decided to contain the possible note durations to whole notes, half notes, quarter notes, eighth notes, and sixteenth notes. A relatively high emotion density is represented by many notes, whereas a relatively low emotion density is represented by fewer notes. We first split the interval between the maximum and minimum emotion density for the novel into five equal parts (five being the number of note duration choices – whole, half, quarter, eighth, or sixteenth). Emotion densities that fall in the lowest interval are mapped to a single whole note. Emotion densities in the next interval are mapped to two half-notes. The next interval is mapped to four quarter-notes. And so on, until the densities in the last interval are mapped to sixteen sixteenth-notes ($1/16^{\text{th}}$). The result is shorter notes during periods of higher emotional activity (with shorter notes making the piece sound more active), and longer notes during periods of lower emotional activity.

Pitch: If the number of notes for a measure is n, then the corresponding sub-section is partitioned into n equal parts and the pitch for each note is based on the emotion density of the corresponding sub-section. Lower emotion densities are mapped to more consonant pitches in the key (C major or C minor), whereas higher emotion densities are mapped to less consonant pitches in the same scale. For example, if the melody is in the key of C major, then the lowest to highest emotion densities are mapped linearly to the pitches C, G, E, A, D, F, B. Thus, a low emotion value would create a pitch that is more consonant and a high emotion value would create a pitch that is more dissonant (more interesting and unusual).

Repetition: Once the four measures of a section are played, the same four measures are repeated in order to create a more structured and melodic feeling. Without the repetition, the piece sounds less cohesive.

6.4 Tempo

We use a $\frac{4}{4}$ time signature (common time) because it is one of the most popular time signatures. Thus each measure (sub-section) has 4 beats. We determined tempo (beats per minute) by first determining how active the target novel is. Each of the eight basic emotions is assigned to be either active, passive, or neutral. In TransProse, the tempo is proportional to the *activity score*, which we define to be the difference between the average density of the active emotions (anger and joy) and the average density of the passive emotions (sadness). The other five emotions (anticipation, disgust, fear, surprise, and trust) were considered ambiguous or neutral, and did not influence the tempo.

We subjectively identified upper and lower bounds for the possible tempo values to be 180 and 40 beats/minute, respectively. We determined activity scores for a collection of novels, and identified the highest activity score (Act_{max}) and the lowest activity score (Act_{min}). For a novel whose activity score was Act, we determined tempo as per the formula shown below:

$$tempo = 40 + \frac{(Act - Act_{min}) * (180 - 40)}{Act_{max} - Act_{min}} \quad (3)$$

Thus, high activity scores were represented by

tempo values closer to 180 and lower activity scores were represented by tempo values closer to 40. The lowest activity score in our collection of texts, Act_{min}, was -0.002 whereas the highest activity score, Act_{max}, was 0.017.

7 Converting Specifications to Music

JFugue is an open-source Java API that helps create generative music.[7] It allows the user to easily experiment with different notes, instruments, octaves, note durations, etc within a Java program. JFugue requires a line of specifically-formatted text that describes the melodies in order to play them. The initial portion of the string of JFugue tokens for the novel *Peter Pan* is shown below. The string conveys the overall information of the piece as well as the first eight measures (or one section) for each of the three melodies (or voices).

> KCmaj X[VOLUME]=16383 V0 T180 A6/0.25 D6/0.125 F6/0.25 B6/0.25 B6/0.125 B6/0.25 B6/0.25...

K stands for key and *Cmaj* stands for C major. This indicates that the rest of the piece will be in the key of C major. The second token controls the volume, which in this example is at the loudest value (16383). *V0* stands for the first melody (or voice). The tokens with the letter T indicate the tempo, which in the case of this example is 180 beats per minute.

The tokens that follow indicate the notes of the melody. The letter is the pitch class of the note, and the number immediately following it is the octave. The number following the slash character indicates the duration of the note. (0.125 is an eighth-note (1/8th), 0.25 is a quarter note, 0.5 is a half note, and 1.0 is a whole note.) We used JFugue to convert the specifications of the melodies into music. JFugue saves the pieces as a midi files, which we converted to MP3 format.[8]

8 Case Studies

We created musical pieces for several popular novels through TransProse. These pieces are available at: `http://transprose.weebly.com/final-pieces.html`. Since these novels are likely to have been read by many people, the readers can compare their understanding of the story with the music generated by TransProse. Table 1 presents details of some of these novels.

8.1 Overall Tone

TransProse captures the overall positive or negative tone of the novel by assigning an either major or minor key to the piece. *Peter Pan* and *Anne of Green Gables*, novels with overall happy and uplifting moods, created pieces in the major key. On the other hand, novels such as *Heart of Darkness, A Clockwork Orange*, and *The Road*, with dark themes, created pieces in the minor key. The effect of this is pieces that from the start have a mood that aligns with the basic mood of the novel they are based on.

8.2 Overall Happiness and Sadness

The densities of happiness and sadness in a novel are represented in the baseline octave of a piece. This representation instantly conveys whether the novel has a markedly happy or sad mood. The overall high happiness densities in *Peter Pan* and *Anne of Green Gables* create pieces in an octave above the average, resulting in higher tones and a lighter overall mood. Similarly, the overall high sadness densities in *The Road* and *Heart of Darkness* result in pieces an octave lower than the average, and a darker overall tone to the music. Novels, such as *A Clockwork Orange*, and *The Little Prince*, where happiness and sadness are not dramatically higher or lower than the average novel remain at the average octave, allowing for the creation of a more nuanced piece.

8.3 Activeness of the Novel

Novels with lots of active emotion words, such as *Peter Pan, Anne of Green Gables, Lord of the Flies,* and *A Clockwork Orange*, generate fast-paced pieces with tempos over 170 beats per minute. On the other hand, *The Road*, which has relatively few active emotion words is rather slow (a tempo of 42 beats per minute).

8.4 Primary Emotions

The top two emotions of a novel inform two of the three melodies in a piece (M_{e1} and M_{e2}). Recall that if the melody is based on a positive emotion, it will be an octave higher than the octave of M_o, and if it is based on a negative emotion, it will be an octave lower. For novels where the top two emotions

[7] `http://www.jfugue.org`

[8] The MP3 format uses a lossy data compression, but the resulting files are significantly smaller in size. Further, a wider array of music players support the MP3 format.

Table 1: Emotion and audio features of a few popular novels that were processed by TransProse. The musical pieces are available at: http://transprose.weebly.com/final-pieces.html.

Book Title	Emotion 1	Emotion 2	Octave	Tempo	Pos/Neg	Key	Activity	Joy-Sad
A Clockwork Orange	Fear	Sadness	5	171	Negative	C Minor	0.009	-0.0007
Alice in Wonderland	Trust	Fear	5	150	Positive	C Major	0.007	-0.0002
Anne of Green Gables	Joy	Trust	6	180	Positive	C Major	0.010	0.0080
Heart of Darkness	Fear	Sadness	4	122	Negative	C Minor	0.005	-0.0060
Little Prince, The	Trust	Joy	5	133	Positive	C Major	0.006	0.0028
Lord of The Flies	Fear	Sadness	4	151	Negative	C Minor	0.008	-0.0053
Peter Pan	Trust	Joy	6	180	Positive	C Major	0.010	0.0040
Road, The	Sadness	Fear	4	42	Negative	C Minor	-0.002	-0.0080
To Kill a Mockingbird	Trust	Fear	5	132	Positive	C Major	0.006	-0.0013

are both positive, such as *Anne of Green Gables* (trust and joy), the pieces sound especially light and joyful. For novels where the top two emotions are both negative, such as *The Road* (sadness and fear), the pieces sound especially dark.

8.5 Emotional Activity

Unlike the overall pace of the novel, individual segments of activity were also identified in the pieces through the number and duration of notes (with more and shorter notes indicating higher emotion densities). This can be especially heard in the third section of *A Clockwork Orange*, the final section of *The Adventures of Sherlock Holmes*, the second section of *To Kill a Mockingbird*, and the final section of *Lord of the Flies*. In *A Clockwork Orange*, the main portion of the piece is chaotic and eventful, likely as the main characters cause havoc; at the end of the novel (as the main character undergoes therapy) the piece dramatically changes and becomes structured. Similarly, in *Heart of Darkness*, the piece starts out only playing a few notes; as the tension in the novel builds, the number of notes increases and their durations decrease.

9 Comparing Alternative Choices

We examine choices made in TransProse by comparing musical pieces generated with different alternatives. These audio clips are available here: http://transprose.weebly.com/clips.html.

Pieces with two melodies (based on overall emotion density and the predominant emotion's density) and pieces based on four melodies (based on the top three emotions and the overall emotion density) were generated and uploaded in the clips webpage. Observe that with only two melodies, the pieces tend to sound thin, whereas with four melodies the pieces sound less cohesive and sometimes chaotic. The effect of increasing and decreasing the total number of sections and subsections is also presented. Additionally, the webpage displays pieces with tempos and octaves beyond the limits chosen in TransProse. We also show other variations such as pieces for relatively positive novels generated in C minor (instead of C major). These alternatives are not necessarily incorrect, but they tend to often be less effective.

10 Limitations and Future work

We presented a system, TransProse, that generates music according to the use of emotion words in a given piece of text. A number of avenues for future work exist such as exploring the use of mid-piece key changes and intentional harmony and discord between the melodies. We will further explore ways to capture activity in music. For example, an automatically generated activity lexicon (built using the method proposed by Turney and Littman (2003)) can be used to identify portions of text where the characters are relatively active (fighting, dancing, conspiring, etc) and areas where they are relatively passive (calm, incapacitated, sad, etc). One can even capture non-emotional features of the text in music. For example, recurring characters or locations in a novel could be indicated by recurring motifs. We will conduct human evaluations asking people to judge various aspects of the generated music such as the quality of music and the amount and type of emotion evoked by the music. We will also evaluate the impact of textual features such as the length of the novel and the style of writing on the generated music. Work on capturing note models (analogous to language models) from existing pieces of music and using them to improve the music generated by TransProse seems especially promising.

References

[Agarwal et al.2011] Apoorv Agarwal, Boyi Xie, Ilia Vovsha, Owen Rambow, and Rebecca Passonneau. 2011. Sentiment analysis of twitter data. In *Proceedings of the Workshop on Languages in Social Media*, LSM '11, pages 30–38, Portland, Oregon.

[Aisopos et al.2012] Fotis Aisopos, George Papadakis, Konstantinos Tserpes, and Theodora Varvarigou. 2012. Textual and contextual patterns for sentiment analysis over microblogs. In *Proceedings of the 21st International Conference on World Wide Web Companion*, WWW '12 Companion, pages 453–454, New York, NY, USA.

[Ali and Peynirciolu2010] S Omar Ali and Zehra F Peynirciolu. 2010. Intensity of emotions conveyed and elicited by familiar and unfamiliar music. *Music Perception: An Interdisciplinary Journal*, 27(3):177–182.

[Alm and Sproat2005] Cecilia O. Alm and Richard Sproat, 2005. *Emotional sequencing and development in fairy tales*, pages 668–674. Springer.

[Aman and Szpakowicz2007] Saima Aman and Stan Szpakowicz. 2007. Identifying expressions of emotion in text. In Vclav Matoušek and Pavel Mautner, editors, *Text, Speech and Dialogue*, volume 4629 of *Lecture Notes in Computer Science*, pages 196–205. Springer Berlin / Heidelberg.

[Bakliwal et al.2012] Akshat Bakliwal, Piyush Arora, Senthil Madhappan, Nikhil Kapre, Mukesh Singh, and Vasudeva Varma. 2012. Mining sentiments from tweets. In *Proceedings of the 3rd Workshop on Computational Approaches to Subjectivity and Sentiment Analysis*, WASSA '12, pages 11–18, Jeju, Republic of Korea.

[Balkwill and Thompson1999] Laura-Lee Balkwill and William Forde Thompson. 1999. A cross-cultural investigation of the perception of emotion in music: Psychophysical and cultural cues. *Music perception*, pages 43–64.

[Bellegarda2010] Jerome Bellegarda. 2010. Emotion analysis using latent affective folding and embedding. In *Proceedings of the NAACL-HLT 2010 Workshop on Computational Approaches to Analysis and Generation of Emotion in Text*, Los Angeles, California.

[Biles1994] John Biles. 1994. Genjam: A genetic algorithm for generating jazz solos. pages 131–137.

[Bollen et al.2009] Johan Bollen, Alberto Pepe, and Huina Mao. 2009. Modeling public mood and emotion: Twitter sentiment and socio-economic phenomena. *CoRR*.

[Boucouvalas2002] Anthony C. Boucouvalas. 2002. Real time text-to-emotion engine for expressive internet communication. *Emerging Communication: Studies on New Technologies and Practices in Communication*, 5:305–318.

[Brody and Diakopoulos2011] Samuel Brody and Nicholas Diakopoulos. 2011. Cooooooooooooooollllllllllllll!!!!!!!!!!!!!!: using word lengthening to detect sentiment in microblogs. In *Proceedings of the Conference on Empirical Methods in Natural Language Processing*, EMNLP '11, pages 562–570, Stroudsburg, PA, USA. Association for Computational Linguistics.

[Brown1970] Calvin S Brown. 1970. The relations between music and literature as a field of study. *Comparative Literature*, 22(2):97–107.

[Collins2008] Nick Collins. 2008. The analysis of generative music programs. *Organised Sound*, 13(3):237–248.

[Cope1996] David Cope. 1996. *Experiments in musical intelligence*, volume 12. AR Editions Madison, WI.

[Dowling and Harwood1986] W Jay Dowling and Dane L Harwood. 1986. *Music cognition*, volume 19986. Academic Press New York.

[Gabrielsson and Lindström2001] Alf Gabrielsson and Erik Lindström. 2001. The influence of musical structure on emotional expression.

[Genereux and Evans2006] Michel Genereux and Roger P. Evans. 2006. Distinguishing affective states in weblogs. In *Proceedings of the AAAI Spring Symposium on Computational Approaches to Analysing Weblogs*, pages 27–29, Stanford, California.

[Hatten1991] Robert Hatten. 1991. On narrativity in music: expressive genres and levels of discourse in beethoven.

[Hunter et al.2008] Patrick G Hunter, E Glenn Schellenberg, and Ulrich Schimmack. 2008. Mixed affective responses to music with conflicting cues. *Cognition & Emotion*, 22(2):327–352.

[Hunter et al.2010] Patrick G Hunter, E Glenn Schellenberg, and Ulrich Schimmack. 2010. Feelings and perceptions of happiness and sadness induced by music: Similarities, differences, and mixed emotions. *Psychology of Aesthetics, Creativity, and the Arts*, 4(1):47.

[Iida et al.2000] Akemi Iida, Nick Campbell, Soichiro Iga, Fumito Higuchi, and Michiaki Yasumura. 2000. A speech synthesis system with emotion for assisting communication. In *ISCA Tutorial and Research Workshop (ITRW) on Speech and Emotion*.

[Juslin and Laukka2003] Patrik N Juslin and Petri Laukka. 2003. Communication of emotions in vocal expression and music performance: Different channels, same code? *Psychological bulletin*, 129(5):770.

[Kim et al.2009] Elsa Kim, Sam Gilbert, Michael J. Edwards, and Erhardt Graeff. 2009. Detecting sadness in 140 characters: Sentiment analysis of mourning michael jackson on twitter.

[Lerdahl and Jackendoff1983] Fred Lerdahl and Ray S Jackendoff. 1983. *A generative theory of tonal music*. MIT press.

[Liu and Zhang2012] Bing Liu and Lei Zhang. 2012. A survey of opinion mining and sentiment analysis. In Charu C. Aggarwal and ChengXiang Zhai, editors, *Mining Text Data*, pages 415–463. Springer.

[Liu et al.2003] Hugo Liu, Henry Lieberman, and Ted Selker. 2003. A model of textual affect sensing using real-world knowledge. In *Proceedings of the 8th International Conference on Intelligent User Interfaces*, pages 125–132, New York, NY. ACM.

[Micznik2001] Vera Micznik. 2001. Music and narrative revisited: degrees of narrativity in beethoven and mahler. *Journal of the Royal Musical Association*, 126(2):193–249.

[Mihalcea and Liu2006] Rada Mihalcea and Hugo Liu. 2006. A corpus-based approach to finding happiness. In *Proceedings of the AAAI Spring Symposium on Computational Approaches to Analysing Weblogs*, pages 139–144. AAAI Press.

[Mohammad and Turney2010] Saif M. Mohammad and Peter D. Turney. 2010. Emotions evoked by common words and phrases: Using Mechanical Turk to create an emotion lexicon. In *Proceedings of the NAACL-HLT Workshop on Computational Approaches to Analysis and Generation of Emotion in Text*, LA, California.

[Mohammad and Turney2013] Saif M. Mohammad and Peter D. Turney. 2013. Crowdsourcing a word-emotion association lexicon. 29(3):436–465.

[Mohammad and Yang2011] Saif M. Mohammad and Tony (Wenda) Yang. 2011. Tracking sentiment in mail: How genders differ on emotional axes. In *Proceedings of the ACL Workshop on Computational Approaches to Subjectivity and Sentiment Analysis*, WASSA '11, Portland, OR, USA.

[Mohammad2012] Saif M. Mohammad. 2012. From once upon a time to happily ever after: Tracking emotions in mail and books. *Decision Support Systems*, 53(4):730–741.

[Morrison and Demorest2009] Steven J Morrison and Steven M Demorest. 2009. Cultural constraints on music perception and cognition. *Progress in brain research*, 178:67–77.

[Neviarouskaya et al.2009] Alena Neviarouskaya, Helmut Prendinger, and Mitsuru Ishizuka. 2009. Compositionality principle in recognition of fine-grained emotions from text. In *Proceedings of the Proceedings of the Third International Conference on Weblogs and Social Media (ICWSM-09)*, pages 278–281, San Jose, California.

[Pak and Paroubek2010] Alexander Pak and Patrick Paroubek. 2010. Twitter as a corpus for sentiment analysis and opinion mining. In *Proceedings of the 7th Conference on International Language Resources and Evaluation*, LREC '10, Valletta, Malta, May. European Language Resources Association (ELRA).

[Pang and Lee2008] Bo Pang and Lillian Lee. 2008. Opinion mining and sentiment analysis. *Foundations and Trends in IR*, 2(1–2):1–135.

[Perricone2000] J. Perricone. 2000. *Melody in Songwriting: Tools and Techniques for Writing Hit Songs*. Berklee guide. Berklee Press.

[Picard2000] Rosalind W Picard. 2000. *Affective computing*. MIT press.

[Pierre-Yves2003] Oudeyer Pierre-Yves. 2003. The production and recognition of emotions in speech: features and algorithms. *International Journal of Human-Computer Studies*, 59(1):157–183.

[Roederer2008] Juan G Roederer. 2008. *The physics and psychophysics of music: an introduction*. Springer Publishing Company, Incorporated.

[Rousseau2009] Jean-Jacques Rousseau. 2009. *Essay on the origin of languages and writings related to music*, volume 7. UPNE.

[Schröder2009] Marc Schröder. 2009. Expressive speech synthesis: Past, present, and possible futures. In *Affective information processing*, pages 111–126. Springer.

[Spencer1857] Herbert Spencer. 1857. The origin and function of music. *Frasers Magazine*, 56:396–408.

[Strapparava and Valitutti2004] Carlo Strapparava and Alessandro Valitutti. 2004. WordNet-Affect: An Affective Extension of WordNet. In *Proceedings of the 4th International Conference on Language Resources and Evaluation (LREC-2004)*, pages 1083–1086, Lisbon, Portugal.

[Tao and Tan2005] Jianhua Tao and Tieniu Tan. 2005. Affective computing: A review. In *Affective computing and intelligent interaction*, pages 981–995. Springer.

[Tenney1988] James Tenney. 1988. *A history of consonance and dissonance*. Excelsior Music Publishing Company New York.

[Thelwall et al.2011] Mike Thelwall, Kevan Buckley, and Georgios Paltoglou. 2011. Sentiment in Twitter events. *Journal of the American Society for Information Science and Technology*, 62(2):406–418.

[Tumasjan et al.2010] Andranik Tumasjan, Timm O Sprenger, Philipp G Sandner, and Isabell M Welpe. 2010. Predicting elections with twitter : What 140 characters reveal about political sentiment. *Word Journal Of The International Linguistic Association*, pages 178–185.

[Turney and Littman2003] Peter Turney and Michael L Littman. 2003. Measuring praise and criticism: Inference of semantic orientation from association. *ACM Transactions on Information Systems*, 21(4).

[Volkova et al.2010] Ekaterina P Volkova, Betty J Mohler, Detmar Meurers, Dale Gerdemann, and Heinrich H Bülthoff. 2010. Emotional perception of fairy tales: Achieving agreement in emotion annotation of text. In *Proceedings of the NAACL HLT 2010 Workshop on Computational Approaches to Analysis and Generation of Emotion in Text*, pages 98–106. Association for Computational Linguistics.

[Webster and Weir2005] Gregory D Webster and Catherine G Weir. 2005. Emotional responses to music: Interactive effects of mode, texture, and tempo. *Motivation and Emotion*, 29(1):19–39.

[Zhe and Boucouvalas2002] Xu Zhe and A Boucouvalas, 2002. *Text-to-Emotion Engine for Real Time Internet CommunicationText-to-Emotion Engine for Real Time Internet Communication*, pages 164–168.

Computational analysis to explore authors' depiction of characters

Joseph Bullard
Dept. of Computer Science
Rochester Institute of Technology
jtb4478@cs.rit.edu

Cecilia Ovesdotter Alm
Dept. of English
Rochester Institute of Technology
coagla@rit.edu

Abstract

This study involves automatically identifying the sociolinguistic characteristics of fictional characters in plays by analyzing their written "speech". We discuss three binary classification problems: predicting the characters' gender (male vs. female), age (young vs. old), and socio-economic standing (upper-middle class vs. lower class). The text corpus used is an annotated collection of August Strindberg and Henrik Ibsen plays, translated into English, which are in the public domain. These playwrights were chosen for their known attention to relevant socio-economic issues in their work. Linguistic and textual cues are extracted from the characters' lines (turns) for modeling purposes. We report on the dataset as well as the performance and important features when predicting each of the sociolinguistic characteristics, comparing intra- and inter-author testing.

1 Introduction

A speech community has sociolinguistic properties. Social variables influencing verbal interaction include, for example, geographical background, gender, age, ethnicity, and class. Writers and playwrights, in turn, use their knowledge of social verbal markers to generate credible and compelling characters. The focus of this study is the creation of an annotated dataset and computational model for predicting the social-biographical aspects of fictional characters based on features of their written "speech" in dramatic plays. The plays used here are authored by August Strindberg and Henrik Ibsen, two Scandinavian playwrights known for creating characters and stories that acted as social commentary and were controversial when they were first written. These authors are also recognized for their contributions in shaping modern drama. Their attention to social issues makes these plays and characters highly relevant in constructing such a model to shed light on how these authors' translated texts portray social variables. Interlocutors' social attributes (such as their gender, age, social class, and ethnicity) are known to correlate with language behavior, and they tap into dimensions of language behavior that are of central interest to the humanities. For instance, anecdotal evidence suggests that large-scale corpus analysis can show how society collectively ascribes certain roles to male versus female referents in text (cf. Lindquist, 2009).

Studying these authors and texts from the point of view of corpus-oriented computational sociolinguistics can also help us examine the authors' differences in production, descriptively. This is useful as a complementary approach to the more traditional close reading methodology common in literary research, through which their texts are usually approached. On a broader scale, the study can contribute valuable insights to a theory of linguistic text criticism. These authors are part of a global literary canon, and their plays are arguably more often performed in translation than in their Scandinavian originals. Accordingly, we focus on analyzing texts translated into English.

We focus on sociolinguistic characteristics that are assigned to each character and that can be described as translating into three binary classification problems: predicting the characters' gender (*male* vs. *female*), age (*young* vs. *old*), and socioeconomic standing or class (*upper-middle class* vs. *lower class*). The text corpus is annotated by assigning each of the characters that match specified criteria a value in each of the characteristics. We do this at the character level, joining all dialogic lines of a character into one instance. The work was accomplished through the use of computational tools for natural language processing, including Python (http://www.python.org/), the Natural Language Toolkit (http://www.nltk.org/) for part of the preprocessing, and the `scikit-learn` machine learning library for the computational modeling. Translated texts that reside in the public domain were collected from the Gutenberg Archive (http://www.gutenburg.org/wiki/Main_Page/).

2 Previous Work

A pilot study by Hota et al. (2006) on automatic gender identification in Shakespeare's texts, as well as a few primarily gender-oriented studies surveyed in Garera and Yarowsky (2009), have set the stage for further inquiry. The latter study expanded on previous work by exploring three attributes: gender, age, and native/non-native speakers. There have been previous avenues of research into categorizing speakers based on different individual sociolinguistic factors. However, not many studies have attempted this categorization with fictional characters. Literary texts are complex, reflecting authors' decision-making and creative processes. From the perspective of digital humanities, such a focus complements computational sociolinguistic modeling of contemporary user-generated text types (such as emails, or blogs (Rosenthal and McKeown, 2011)). As Lindquist (2009) points out, social data for interlocutors is less often attached to openly available linguistic corpora, and interest is strong in developing corpus methods to help explore social language behavior (see Lindquist (2009) and Baker (2010)).

Previous investigation into social dimensions of language has established strong links between language and social attributes of speech communities (for an overview, see Mesthrie et al. (2009)). However, such inquiry has generally had a firm foundation in field-based research and has usually focused on one or just a few linguistic variables (such as how the pronunciation of certain sounds aligns with social stratification (Labov, 1972)). Moreover, previous scholarship has chiefly focused on the spoken rather than the written mode. Garera and Yarowsky (2009) and Boulis and Ostendorf (2005) take into account the interlocutors' speech for analysis. In contrast, we experiment with the challenge of using only sociolinguistically relevant knowledge coded in the text of characters' lines. Thus, our approach is more similar to Hota et al.'s (2006) work on Shakespeare. The characters' lines do not include the metadata needed for considering spoken features, since usually these are added at the discretion of the performer. This may make our problem more challenging, since some of these indicators may be reliable for identifying gender, such as backchannel responses and affirmations from females, and assertively "holding the floor" with filled pauses from males (Boulis and Ostendorf, 2005). Moreover, there are prosodic features that clearly differ between males and females due to physical characteristics (e.g. F_0, predominant for pitch perception). We do not take advantage of acoustic/prosodic cues in this work. Our text is also artificial discourse, as opposed to natural speech; therefore these characters' lines may rather express how writers choose to convey sociolinguistic attributes of their characters.

In terms of features, we have explored observations from previous studies. For instance, common lexical items have been shown successful, with males tending to use more obscenities, especially when talking to other males (Boulis and Ostendorf, 2005), and females tending to use more third-person pronouns. Phrases also tended to be more useful than unigrams, though whether the commonly-used words tend to be content-bearing remains a question according to Boulis and Ostendorf (2005). Tackling another form of text, Kao and Jurafksy (2012) examined the statistical properties of 20th century acknowledged versus amateur poets in terms of style and content substance, finding, for example, that lexical affluence and properties coherent with imagism, as an aesthetic theorized ideal, distinguished contemporary professionals' poetics, while sound phenomena played a lesser role, and amateurs preferred the use of more explicit negative vocabulary than professionals. In our study, we focus on data collection, corpus analysis, and exploratory experimentation with classification algorithms.

3 Data

The texts used were freely available transcriptions from the Gutenberg Archive. English translations of public-domain plays by August Strindberg and Henrik Ibsen were collected from the archive, from various translators and years of release. As noted above, these plays are often performed in English, and we assume that the translations will convey relevant linguistic cues, as influenced by

	Strindberg	Ibsen	**Total**
# of plays	11	12	**23**
# of characters	65	93	**158**
# of lines	6555	12306	**18861**

Table 1: Distribution of plays, characters, and lines between Strindberg and Ibsen in the dataset.

Character	Gender	Age	Class
Christine	Female	Young	Upper
Jean	Male	Young	Lower
Miss Julia	Female	Young	Lower

Table 2: Example annotations from *Miss Julia*.

authors, as well as translators. We assume that the translators intended to replicate as closely as possible the voice of the original author, as this is generally the function of literary translation, but we recognize the potential for loss of information.

The texts were minimally pre-processed (such as removing licensing and introduction text), leaving only the written lines-to-be-spoken of the characters. Each character's lines were automatically extracted and aggregated using a Python script. Characters should have a significant number of lines (equal to or greater than fifteen in his or her respective play) to be considered.[1] We also record metadata per character, such as the play title, the play translator, and the URL of the original play text on Gutenberg. The basic characteristics of the resulting dataset are shown in Table 1.

In terms of annotation, characters from each play were annotated by a third party and assigned characteristics primarily according to the plot descriptions on Wikipedia of their respective plays of origin. The characteristics considered were gender (male vs. female), age (young vs. old), and socioeconomic standing or class (upper-middle class vs. lower class). For example, for *age*, characters with children are considered *old*, and those children are considered *young*. A childless character whose peers have children or who has experienced life-changing events typically associated with age (e.g. widows/widowers) is also *old*, unless separately noted otherwise. The *gender* annotations were validated by a project-independent person

[1]The only exception to this rule is Mrs. X from Strindberg's *The Stronger*. She has only 11 separate "lines", but also has the only speaking part for the entire play, which is a single act of substantial length. We also note that while an ad hoc threshold for lines was used, future work could explore principled ways to set it.

Attribute	Annotation	Strindberg	Ibsen
Gender	Male / Female	42 / 23	61 / 32
Age	Old / Young	46 / 19	61 / 32
Class	Upper / Lower	57 / 8	83 / 10

Table 3: Character attribute distributions for *gender*, *age*, and *class* for each author.

in Scandinavia (Swedish native speaker) based on her knowledge of Scandinavian naming conventions. Example character annotations for Strindberg's well-known naturalistic play *Miss Julia* (or *Miss Julie*) are shown in Table 2. As seen in Table 3, the imbalance of *class* labels presents the greatest problem for our model. Baselines of 88% and 89% *upper class* for Strindberg and Ibsen, respectively, indicate that there may be less information to be extracted for *class*.

4 Models

Here we describe the design and performance of computational models for predicting a character's *gender*, *age*, and *class* for Strindberg and Ibsen, yielding six models in total. Logistic regression, implemented in Python with the `scikit-learn` machine learning library (Pedregosa et al., 2011), is used for all classification models.

4.1 Feature Extraction

Many features were examined, some inspired by previous analyses in the literature, such as type-token ratio, subordinate clauses, and *wh*-questions, as well as some exploratory features, such as honorific terms of address. A full list of the features examined is shown in Table 4. All features were automatically extracted using Python. We use *honorifics* here to mean common formal terms of address during the time period (*sir, madam, lord, Mr., Mrs.,* etc.). It seems intuitive that such terms may be used differently based on *class* or possibly *age* (e.g. lower class using more higher terms of address when speaking to their superiors). We use *family* words to mean anything that indicates a familial relationship (*father, daughter, nephew,* etc.). The use of such words may be affected by gender roles (Hota et al., 2006). Part-of-speech tagging was accomplished using the Natural Language Toolkit (NLTK) (Bird et al., 2009).

Linguistic features	
Family words	For/with
Honorifics	Modals
Pronouns 1st	Personal pronouns
Pronouns 2nd	Nouns singular
Pronouns 3rd	Nouns plural
Pronouns all	Verbs past
Wh- questions	Verbs past part.
Type-token ratio	Verbs sing. pres. non-3rd
Determiners	Mean line length
Adjectives	Number of lines
Prepositions	% short lines ($\leq$5 words)

Table 4: List of linguistic features examined for the models. All features, with the exception of the last three in the right column, were measured once as raw counts and once as the fraction of the overall words for a given character.

4.2 Cross-Author Validation

We compared translations of Strindberg and Ibsen's use of language to convey sociolinguistic attributes. This was done for each of the three attributes of interest (*gender*, *age*, and *class*) by training one model for each author, then using it to classify the other author's characters. We accomplish this by defining a *cross-author validation* procedure, a variation of the standard k-fold cross-validation procedure in which the trained model in each fold is used to predict both its own test set and the test set of the other author. This procedure is explained visually in Figure 1. The procedure is especially interesting as these two authors were contemporaries and dealt with topics of social commentary in their works, although from their own perspectives.

The results of cross-author validation are shown in Table 5 as a matrix where the row is the author used for training, the column is the author used for testing, and the value inside a cell is the average accuracy over all iterations of cross-author validation. Majority class baselines are also shown. As expected, the models for each author's texts were better at predicting themselves than the other author, with a couple of exceptions. For *age*, the Strindberg-trained model was still able to improve on Ibsen's baseline, but not vice versa. One possible explanation could be that common features between their depictions of *age* might be more useful for one author than the other. Another interesting exception is in the *class* models

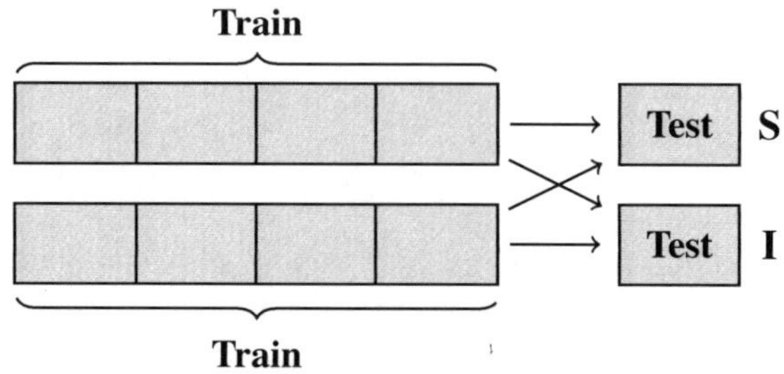

Figure 1: Example of one fold of *cross-author validation* for Strindberg (S) and Ibsen (I). Arrows indicate testing. Each author has its own 5-fold cross-validation, but in each fold, the trained model is tested on both its own test set and the test set of the other author.

	Gender		Age		Class	
	S	I	S	I	S	I
Strindberg (S)	**68**	60	**74**	**70**	**89**	**90**
Ibsen (I)	61	**67**	70	**74**	**91**	**90**
Baseline	65	66	71	66	88	89

Table 5: Results of cross-author validation (see Figure 1). Rows are the author used for training, columns are the author used for testing, and the value in the cell is the average accuracy over 500 iterations of 5-fold cross-validation. Accuracies above majority class baselines are shown in bold.

for both authors, which performed slightly above high baselines for the opposite authors as well as their own. While *class* improvements are recognizably marginal (and not claimed to be significant), these results might indicate that the two authors' translated texts are using similar characteristics to convey social class of their characters. It is important to note that the baselines for *class* were extremely high, making prediction of this attribute more difficult. At least in the intra-author testing, the *gender* and *age* models were generally able to improve accuracy over their respective baselines more so than the *class* models, with *age* being the best overall.

4.3 Comparison of Useful Features

Since the experimentation used a linear model (logistic regression), we can inspect the coefficients/weights of a trained classifier to determine which features contributed particularly to the classification. The absolute value of a coefficient indicates how influential its feature is, and the sign (+/-) of the coefficient indicates which class the feature is associated with. During cross-author

	Strindberg		Ibsen	
Gender	**Pronouns 3rd**	**Female**	**Pronouns 3rd**	**Female**
	Honorifics	Female	Family words	Female
	Determiners	Male	Modals	Male
Age	Nouns singular	Old	**Family words**	**Young**
	Family words	**Young**	Verbs sing. pres. non-3rd	Young
	Modals	Young	Prepositions	Old
Class	**For/with**	**Lower**	**For/with**	**Lower**
	Verbs past part.	Upper	**Honorifics**	**Lower**
	Honorifics	**Lower**	Nouns singular	Lower

Table 6: Most useful features for *gender*, *age*, and *class* for each author, determined by examining the coefficients of classifiers that performed above baseline during cross-author testing. The pairs in the table consist of a linguistic feature and the label indicated by more frequent use of that feature (e.g. for Strindberg, third-person pronoun usage contributed to predicting gender, with greater usage indicating a female character). Features marked in bold are shared between authors for a given attribute.

validation, if the trained classifier for a given fold performed above the baseline of its own test set, then we record its three most heavily weighted features. At the end, we have a tally of which features most often appeared in the top three features for such better-performing classifiers. We can use this to compare which features were more consistently involved for each author and attribute pair, as shown in Table 6.

Some of the useful features are more intuitive than others. For example, as mentioned in an earlier section, it seems reasonable that family words may relate to depictions of gender roles of the time period in which the plays were written, with women being expected to take on social roles more confined to the home. This appears to be true for Ibsen, but not for Strindberg. We also see family words suggesting young characters for both authors' texts. It seems intuitive that authors may have chosen to depict children as spending more time around family members, including using family terminology as terms of address. The use of honorifics is also as predicted earlier in the paper: lower class characters use more higher terms of address, presumably when interacting with their superiors. Another interesting result is the frequency of third-person pronouns being the most useful predictor of gender, indicating female characters for both authors. Possibly, women may have spoken more about other people than men did in these texts.

Some other results are not as easy to explain. For example, the use of the prepositions *for* and *with* was consistently the most useful predictor of lower class characters (which could explain why the models performed comparably on opposite authors in Table 5). An interesting result was the more frequent use of singular, present tense, non-third person verbs among young characters in the Ibsen texts. This suggests that young characters used more verbs centered around *I* and *you* in the present tense. One possible explanation is that children were depicted as being more involved in their own personal world, speaking less about people they were not directly interacting with in a given moment.

5 Conclusion

We have presented a dataset of translated plays by August Strindberg and Henrik Ibsen, along with computational models for predicting the sociolinguistic attributes of gender, age, and social class of characters using the aggregation of their textual lines-to-be-spoken. We compared the performance and important features of the models in both intra- and inter-author testing using a cross-author validation procedure, finding that models generally performed above challenging baselines for their own authors, but less so for the other, as one would expect. The exception was the social class variable, which was consistently slightly above baseline regardless of the author used for testing. While this could indicate that the translated Strindberg and Ibsen texts conveyed social class using similar linguistic cues, this remains a topic for future exploration, given the class imbalance for that attribute. We also examine some indicative features for each attribute and author pair, identifying similarities and differences between the depictions in each set of texts. This analysis supported the trends seen in the cross-author testing.

Future work would include exploring other authors and literary genres, or extending the scope to non-literary domains. When expanding this initial work to larger datasets, there is an opportunity to better understand the intricacies of performance through other metrics (e.g. precision, recall). There is certainly much opportunity to expand sociolinguistic features on fictional texts and to explore other potentially simpler or more advanced modeling frameworks. Alternatives for assigning annotation of sociolinguistic variables, such as socioeconomic standing, also deserve further attention. Additionally, it would be interesting to verify the preservation of linguistic/sociolinguistic cues in translation by repeating this work using different translations of the same texts.

Acknowledgements

We thank the Swedish Institute (http://eng.si.se) for partially supporting this work. We also thank the reviewers for valuable comments that were considered in the revision of this paper.

References

Paul Baker. 2010. *Sociolinguistics and Corpus Linguistics*. Edinburgh University Press, Edinburgh.

Steven Bird, Ewan Klein, and Edward Loper. 2009. *Natural Language Processing with Python – Analyzing Text with the Natural Language Toolkit*. O'Reilly Media, Sebastopol.

Constantinos Boulis and Mari Ostendorf. 2005. A quantitative analysis of lexical differences between genders in telephone conversations. In *Proceedings of the 43rd Annual Meeting of the ACL*, pages 435–442, Ann Arbor, MI, USA, June.

Nikesh Garera and David Yarowsky. 2009. Modeling latent biographic attributes in conversational genres. In *Proceedings of the 47th Annual Meeting of the ACL and 4th IJCNLP of the AFNLP*, pages 719–718, Suntec, Singapore, August.

Sobhan Raj Hota, Shlomo Argamon, and Rebecca Chung. 2006. Gender in Shakespeare: Automatic stylistics gender character classification using syntactic, lexical and lemma features. In *Digital Humanities and Computer Science (DHCS 2006)*.

Justine Kao and Dan Jurafsky. 2012. A computational analysis of style, affect, and imagery in contemporary poetry. In *Workshop on Computational Linguistics for Literature*, pages 8–17, Montréal, Canada, June 8.

William Labov. 1972. *Sociolinguistic Patterns*. University of Pennsylvania Press, Philadelphia, PA.

Hans Lindquist. 2009. *Corpus Linguistics and the Description of English*. Edinburgh University Press, Edinburgh.

Rajend Mesthrie, Joan Swann, Anna Deumert, and William Leap. 2009. *Introducing Sociolinguistics (2nd ed.)*. Jon Benjamins, Amsterdam.

Fabian Pedregosa, Gael Varoquaux, Alexandre Gramfort, Vincent Michel, Bertrand Thirion, Olivier Grisel, Mathieu Blondel, Peter Prettenhofer, Ron Weiss, Vincent Dubourg, Jake Vanderplas, Alexandre Passos, David Cournapeau, Matthieu Brucher, Matthieu Perrot, and Edouard Duchesnay. 2011. Scikit-learn: Machine learning in Python. *Journal of Machine Learning Research*, 12:2825–2830.

Sara Rosenthal and Kathleen McKeown. 2011. Age prediction in blogs: A study of style, content, and online behavior in pre- and post-social media generations. In *Proceedings of the 49th Annual Meeting of the Association for Computational Linguistics*, pages 763–772, Portland, Oregon, June 19-24.

Quotations, Relevance and Time Depth: Medieval Arabic Literature in Grids and Networks

Petr Zemánek
Institute of Comparative Linguistics
Charles University, Prague
Czech Republic
petr.zemanek@ff.cuni.cz

Jiří Milička
Institute of Comparative Linguistics
Charles University, Prague
Czech Republic
jiri@milicka.cz

Abstract

This contribution deals with the use of quotations (repeated n-grams) in the works of medieval Arabic literature. The analysis is based on a 420 millions of words historical corpus of Arabic. Based on repeated quotations from work to work, a network is constructed and used for interpretation of various aspects of Arabic literature. Two short case studies are presented, concentrating on the centrality and relevance of individual works, and the analysis of a time depth and resulting impact of a given work in various periods.

1 Quotations and Their Definition

The relevance of individual works in a given literature and the time depth of such relevance are of interest for many reasons. There are many methods that can reveal such relevance.

The current contribution is based on quotation extraction. Quotations, both covert and overt, both from written and oral sources, belong to constitutive features of medieval Arabic literature.

There are genres which heavily depend on establishing credible links among sources, especially the oral ones, where a trusty chain of tradents is crucial for the claims that such chains accompany. Other links may point to the importance of a given work (or its part) and may uncover previously unseen relations within a given literature or a given genre/register, or reveal connections among genres/registers within a given literature. As such, the results are interesting in a wide research range, from linguists or literature theorists to authors interested in the interactions of various subsets of a given literature.

The research on quotations, their extraction and detection is rich in the NLP, but the algorihms used are based mainly on the quotation-marker recognition, e.g. Pareti et al. (2013), Pouliquen et al. (2007) and Fernandes et al. (2011), or on the metadata procesing (e.g. Shi et al. 2010), to name just a few examples. It can be said that most of the contributions focus on issues different from the one described in this contribution and choose a different approach.

Our understanding of quotations in this project is limited to similar strings of words, i.e. the quotations are very close to borrowings or repetition of verbatim or almost verbatim passages. Technically, it can be viewed as an n-gram that is being repeated in at least two works. These repeated n-grams create links that exhibit some hierarchy, e.g. on the chronological line. The only approach known to us that can be paralleled to ours is the one described in Kolak and Schilit (2008) for quotation mining within the Google Books corpus with algorithm searching for verbatim quotations only.

In a different context and without direct inspiration we developed an algorithm that is tolerant to a certain degree of lexical and morphological variation and word order variability. The reason for this tolerance is both the type of the Arabic language (flective morphology and free word order), but also the fact that the quotations in medieval Arabic literature tend not to be very strict. Despite of the fact that the matching is not so rigorous, we assume that the length of n-grams we use drastically decreases possibilities of random matches.

The frequency of such n-gram repetition in various literary works can point to several aspects, however, in this contribution we will limit ourselves to interpreting such links in a rather cautious and not too far-reaching manner, mainly as pointers to the fact that the writer of the book where the quotations appear was also a reader of the book from which the quotations stem and that he was to a certain degree influenced by it.

This does not necessarily mean that the lineage of quotations is complete in our picture, for we have to admit that there could be some author — member of the lineage — who is not involved in our corpus. In our graph, however, edges point to the first instance of a given n-gram in our data.

2 The Data, Its Organization and Extraction

It is obvious that for the type of the task mentioned in the previous chapter, there is a need of an appropriate data set.

2.1 Historical Corpus of Arabic

All the data in this contribution come from a historical corpus of Arabic (CLAUDIA — Corpus LinguæArabicæUniversalis DIAchronicus). This corpus covers all the main phases of the Arabic writings, from the 7th century to mid 20th century C.E. It contains ca. 2 thousand works and ca. 420 million words. The individual works are present in their entirety, i.e. each file contains a full text of a given literary work, based on edited manuscripts. All the main registers (genres) that appeared in the history of Arabic literature are represented in the corpus.

All the texts in the corpus are raw, without additional annotation. The files contain only a basic annotation of parts to be excluded from analyses (introductions, editorial forewords, etc.). This is of importance for the algorithms development, as the ambiguity of a text written down in Arabic letters is rather high (cf. e.g. Beesley 2001, Buckwalter 2004 or Smrž 2007 passim). On the other hand, it is certainly clear that the ambiguity significantly decreases when the n-gram information (i.e. context) is introduced.

As such, the corpus can be viewed as a network-like representation of Arabic literature. Each work is assigned several attributes, such as authorship, position on the time line, genre characteristics, etc. As several of the attributes can be viewed from several angles, it should be made clear that the genre characteristics currently used correspond to rather traditional terms used in Arabic and Islamic studies. Currently, the attributes assigned to the individual works are based on extra-corpus information and all of them were assigned manually from standard sources.

A short remark on the character of Arabic literature is appropriate. One should bear in mind that the approach to literature as consisting only of belles-lettres is relatively new, and for Arabic literature can be applied at the soonest at the end of the 19th century. All the previous phases must be seen as containing very different genres, including science, philosophy, popular reading and poetry as well as a huge bulk of writings connected with Islam, thus representing rather the concept of "Schrifttum" as expressed in the canonical compendia on Arabic literature, such as Brockelmann (last edition 1996). This is also reflected in current contribution, as many of our examples are connected with Islamic literature covering all the aspects of the study of religion. This includes theology, Islamic law, history, evaluation of sources, tradition, etc. Further information can be found e.g. in Kuiper 2010.

2.2 The Grid and the Network

The construction of a grid from a corpus consists basically in defining some constitutive units that serve as nodes. There are several possibilities of constituting such units, but some obvious solutions might not work very well. At first glance, it is advisable to find as small a unit as possible, while still retaining its meaningfulness; we decided to identify such units with individual works, or titles, with possible further division: Arabic literature is full of several-volume sets, and as our analyses showed, it may be sometimes useful to treat them as multi-part units, where individual parts can be treated as individual nodes (e.g., in some of our analyses it appeared that only a second volume of a three-volume set was significant). Treating such parts as individual nodes reveals similar cases instantly and can prevent overlooking important features during the analysis.

The nodes should allow reasonable links leading from one node to another. These links are crucial for any possible interpretation, as they show various types of relations between individual nodes. These nodes can be again grouped together, to show relations among different types of grouped information (i.e. links between titles or their parts, among authors, centuries, genres, etc.).

The nodes as such create the basis for the construction of both the grid and the network. As pointed out, currently the main axes used for grid and network construction are the authorship, chronological line, and the register information. The links among individual nodes are interpreted as relational links, or edges, in a network. These links also reflect quantitative data (currently, the number of quotations normalized to the lengths of the documents). The grid currently consists of the chronological line and the line of the works (documents). Above this grid, a network consisting of edges connecting the works is constructed. The grid in our approach corresponds to a firm frame where some basic attributes are used. The network then consists of the relations that go across the grid and reveal new connections between individual units.

A terminological remark is appropriate here. The network constructed above the grid corresponds to a great deal to what is called a *weighted graph* (the width of edges reflects the frequency of links). The term *directed graph* could also be used, however, in our current conception of the network, the links are not really oriented, as the direction of links pointing to contemporary authors is sometimes not clearly determinable, contrary to authors with greater time gap.[1] That is why we call these links *edges* and not *arcs*, and possibly, the graph could be called a *semi-directed graph.*

Kolak and Schilit (2008) observe that the standard plagiarism detection algorithms are useless for unmarked quotation mining and suggest straightforward and efficient algorithm for repeated passage extraction. The algorithm is suitable for modern English texts, since quotations are more or less verbatim and the word order is stable. But it is insufficient for medieval Arabic texts as the quotations are usually not really strict and the word order in Arabic is variable. We decided that our algorithm must be a) word order insensitive; b) tolerant to certain degree of variability in the content of quotations, so that the algorithm allows some variation introduced by the copyist, and reflects possibilities of change due to the fact that Arabic is a flective language.

2.3 Quotations extraction: technical description

The basic operation in the process is the quotations extraction. The procedure itself could be used in plagiarism detection, however, such labels do not make sense in case of medieval literature with different scales of values.

The quotation extraction process consists of four phases:

[1]Our time reference is based on the date of death of respective authors, and thus can be considered as "raw". Data on the publication of a respective book are often not available for more distant periods.

1. The corpus is prepared for analysis. Numerals and junk characters are removed from the corpus, as well as all other types of noise. Reverse index of all word types in the corpus is constructed (in case of texts written in Arabic script, a special treatment of diacritical signs and the *aliph*-grapheme and its variants is necessary).

2. All repeating n-grams greater than 7 tokens are logged (the algorithm is tolerant to the word order variability and to the variability of types up to 10 %) [2] : Tokens of every n-gram in the text are sorted according to their frequency in the whole corpus (for every n in some reasonable range, in our case $n \in< 7; 200 >$).
   (a) The positions of $round(0.1n) + 1$ least frequent tokens[3] are looked up in the reverse index.
   (b) The neighbourhoods of the positions are tested for being quotations of the length of *n* tokens.
   (c) Quotations are merged so that quotations larger than *n* tokens are detected as well.

3. For each pair of texts i, j the following index $\Xi_{(i,j)}$ is calculated (N is the number of tokens in a text, M is the number of tokens that are part of quotations of the text j in the text i, K is the set of all pairs of texts in the corpus; h is the parameter that determines number of edges visible in the graph, for details see below):

[2]The minimal length of the quotation and the percentage of word types variability should have been determined on an empirical basis, maximizing recall and precision. The problem is that the decision whether the repeating text passage is a quotation or not is not a binary one. Kolak and Schilit (2008) note the problem and let their subjects evaluate results of their algorithm on a 1–5 scale. As we did not manage to do vast and proper evaluation of the outputs of our algorithm using various minimal lengths of the quotations and degrees of variability, we relied on our subjective experience. The minimal length was set so that it exceeds length of the most common Arabic phrases and Islamic eulogies and the percentage of variable words was set to cover some famous examples of formulaicity in Arabic literature

It needs to be said that some minor changes of the parameters do not influence the results excessively, at least for the case studies we present here.

[3]The reason being the 10% tolerance.

$$\Xi_{i,j} = log_2 \frac{h \frac{M_{i,j}}{N_i N_j}}{\sum_{(k,l) \in K} \frac{M_{k,l}}{N_k N_l}}$$

It should be noted that the formula given above is inspired by the Mutual Information but it has no interpretation within the theory of information. It was constructed only to transform the number of quoted tokens into some index that could be graphically represented in some reasonable way convenient to the human mind.

4. The edges representing links with Ξ lower than a certain threshold are omitted. The threshold is set to 0.5 according to the limits of the programs producing graphic representation of the graph (the width of the line representing the edge is associated directly with the index Ξ). The index is normalized by the parameter h so that the user can set density of the graph, i.e. manipulate the index on an ad hoc basis with consideration for suitable number of edges and their ideal average width. E.g., the number of word tokens involved in autoquotations in Qur'an is $13\,956$ and the overall number of tokens is $80\,047$.

$$\frac{M_{Qur'an,Qur'an}}{N_{Qur'an} N_{Qur'an}} = \frac{13\,956}{80\,047^2} = 0.00000218$$

For our corpus, the average value is 0.000025, setting $h < 16.23$ then means that the Qur'anic autoquotation link will not be represented in the graph. Setting $h = 0.346574$ means that an average link gets $\Xi = 0.5$. Setting $h = 2$ means that an average link gets $\Xi = 1$.

The relation is exported to the .dot format and the graph is generated by popular applications GraphViz and GVEdit.[4]

The resulting database is stored in a binary format, but the graphical user interface allows the researchers to export graphs in accordance to their concepts. The features of the graphs can be changed by manipulating the h parameter and some other options. The appearance of the nodes can be freely adjusted as well.

More detailed information on the overall technical process is available directly from the authors.

[4]http://www.graphviz.org

3 The Analysis and Interpretation

The results are currently stored in a database and are available for further analyses. It is clear that results from a corpus of 420 million words offer many ways of interpretation.

The usage of the extracted data is to a certain degree limited in nature. It is mainly suitable for discussion of relations among individual nodes (documents, titles) or their groups. However, further processing of the data will enable a wider palette of possibilities. Currently, and also due to the limitations of this paper, only a few examples will be given.

3.1 Central Nodes and Relevance

The centrality of a given document may point to its relevance for its surroundings. If the relations that were found by our algorithms are interpreted merely as showing influence of predecessors on the author and his influence on his successors, then the number of links to and from an author and his particular book shows the relevance of that book.

In graph theory, there is no general agreement on how centrality should be defined. We expand the large number of indices of the degree centrality with our own index that is based on the same idea as the Ξ index (J is the set of all texts):

$$C_D(i) = \sum_{j \in J} \frac{M_{i,j}}{N_i N_j}$$

The measurement of this rather primitive and straightforward index results in table 1. The table also contains the plain number of edges at $h = 10$ (marked as *edg.*):

As the pointers to the subject of the respective works show, it was not only Islamic subjects that found their way to the most cited works in Arabic literature — historical literature as well as educative literature obviously played an important role in the medieval Arabic civilization.

It is interesting that az-Zayla'i's node comprises only the second volume of his three-volume *Nasab ar-Raya* (*Erection of the Flag*) — the other volumes exhibit either no edges or very few (0–1 and 1–0 respectively and the quotations point to his 2nd volume). Another interesting fact is that az-Zayla'i is rather less-known today — a short reference can be found in Lane 2005: 150 (fn. 2 and 3). This is also confirmed by the situation today. An Internet search for this author (including Arabic sources) yields only a short paragraph on his

	Degree C_D	Cited C_D	Citing C_D	Cited edg.	Citing edg.
1	0.0958	0.0278	0.0681	70	12
2	0.08257	0.0789	0.0036	23	5
3	0.07763	0.0001	0.0775	0	2
4	0.07277	0.0597	0.0130	155	0
5	0.04562	0.0038	0.0418	35	13

Table 1: Texts sorted according to the degree centrality (first five texts). Authors with their works and genre:
1 = az-Zayla'i — *Nasab ar-Raya*, vol. 2 (Islam)
2 = Abu Nu'aym al-Isbahani — *Axbar Isbahan* (history)
3 = Abu Nu'aym al-Isbahani — *Tarix Isbahan* (history)
4 = an-Nasa'i — *Sunna* (Islam)
5 = al-Yafi'i — *Mir'at al-Jinan* (educative literature — adab).

birth (small village in Somalia, no date) and death (Cairo 1360).

Ibn Xaldun (d. 1382) is a very well-known figure today, respected for his *History*. Today, especially his *Introduction* (*Muqaddima*) is appreciated as an insightful methodological propedeutics. In Figure 2, his relevance in the Middle Ages is measured: it comprises 4 volumes: *Introduction* and *History* vols. 1–3. The graph shows (apart from numerous autoquotations) that his 3rd volume is the central one, where most of incoming and outgoing links can be found. On the other hand, his Muqaddima, which is praised today for its originality, remains isolated (our data do not cover the second half of the 20th century, where this appreciation could be found).

3.2 Time Depth

As our network combines a grid with chronological axis, it is rather easy to follow the distribution of links connected to a given node not only the relevance to other nodes, but also in time. As relevance of a given work is mostly judged from our current point of view (i.e. from what is considered important in the 21st century), an unbiased analysis may give interesting results showing both inspirational sources of a given work and its influence on other authors; it can also show the limits of such influence.

Figure 1 concentrates on the figure of az-Zayla'i (d. 1360), who obviously played an important role in transmitting the knowledge (or discussion, at least) between different periods (cf. 3.1). The second volume of his *Nasab ar-Raya* is a clear center of the network.

The dating of the numerous sources that he used while writing his book starts ca. from the 10th century and to a great deal almost ignores 11th and 12th centuries. There is a thick web of links to his contemporaries, and his direct influence is very strong on the authors of the following century, but slowly wanes with the passage of time — although there are some attestations of his influence in the 16th and 17th centuries, they are getting less and less numerous. In the 20th century there are only two authors at whom we found some reflection of az-Zayla'i 's work.

From the point of view of the 21st century, az-Zayla'i is a marginal figure, both for the Western and Arabic civilizations. On the other hand, as our data show, his importance was crucial for the discussion on Islamic themes for several centuries, which is, apart from the data given above, confirmed also by frequent quotations of his name and writings in the titles starting from the 15th century on.[5]

It is appropriate to repeat here that such conclusions can be viewed as mere signals, as we cannot exclude that there is some title occurring in the quotations lineage but missing in our data.

It should also be stressed that these conclusions reflect only verbatim quotations and are not based on the contents of these works. In other words, the relations do not represent an immediate reflection of the spread of ideas of a given author but rather show the usage of a given work in various periods of the evolution of Arabic literature.

4 Future Work

It is clear that there are many ways in which we can continue in our project. In the near future, we plan to work on the following topics:

- experimenting with various lengths of the shortest quotation and the degree of allowed variability, maximizing recall and precision.

[5] The title of the book is attested in other writings in our dataset in the 15–17th centuries only; the name of the author appears abundantly in the 15th century (ca 1050x), 16th century (ca 560x), 17th century (ca 500x). The 18th century gives only 45 occurrences, later on his name can be found only in specialized Islamic treatises.

- enriching the palette of nodes' attributes to enable a broader scope of analyses based both on external sources and inner textual properties of given texts;
- comparison of the complexity of the graphs of various subcorpora organized according to different criteria;
- comparison of various indices of centrality;
- detailed interpretation of edges;
- comparison with other corpora and
- network of autoquotations within one text.

Acknowledgments

The research reflected in this article has been supported by the GAČR (Czech Science Foundation), project no. 13-28220S.

We would also like to thank to the anonymous reviewers for their inspiring comments.

References

Kenneth R. Beesley. 2001. Finite-State Morphological Analysis and Generation of Arabic at Xerox Research: Status and Plans in 2001. *ACL Workshop on Arabic Language Processing: Status and Perspective.* Toulouse, France: 1–8.

Carl Brockelmann. 1996. *Geschichte der Arabischen Literatur,* (4 Volume Set). Brill, Leiden (1st edition: 1923).

Tim Buckwalter. 2004. Issues in Arabic Orthography and Morphology Analysis. *The Workshop on Computational Approaches to Arabic Script-based Languages, COLING.* Geneva: 31–34.

William Paulo Ducca Fernandes, Eduardo Motta and Ruy Luiz Milidiú. 2011. Quotation Extraction for Portuguese. *Proceedings of the 8th Brazilian Symposium in Information and Human Language Technology.* Cuiabá: 204–208.

Okan Kolak and Bill N. Schilit. 2008. Generating Links by Mining Quotations. *HT '08: Proceedings of the nineteenth ACM conference on Hypertext and hypermedia.* New York: 117–126.

Kathleen Kuiper. 2010. *Islamic Art, Literature and Culture.* Rosen Publishing Group.

Andrew J. Lane. 2005. *A Traditional Mu'tazilite Qur'an Commentary: The Kashshaf of Jar Allah al-Zamakhsari (d.538/1144).* Brill, Leiden.

Silvia Pareti, Tim O'Keefe, Ioannis Konstas, James R. Curran and Irena Koprinska. 2013. Automatically Detecting and Attributing Indirect Quotations. *Proceedings of the 2013 Conference on Empirical Methods in Natural Language Processing.* Seattle: 989–999.

Bruno Pouliquen, Ralf Steinberger and Clive Best. 2007. Automatic Detection Of Quotations in Multilingual News. *Proceedings of Recent Advances in Natural Language Processing 2007.* Borovets.

Xiaolin Shi, Jure Leskovec and Daniel A. McFarland. 2010. Citing for High Impact. *Proceedings of the 10th annual joint conference on Digital libraries.* New York: 49–58.

Otakar Smrž. 2007. *Functional Arabic Morphology. Formal System and Implementation.* Doctoral Thesis, Charles University, Prague.

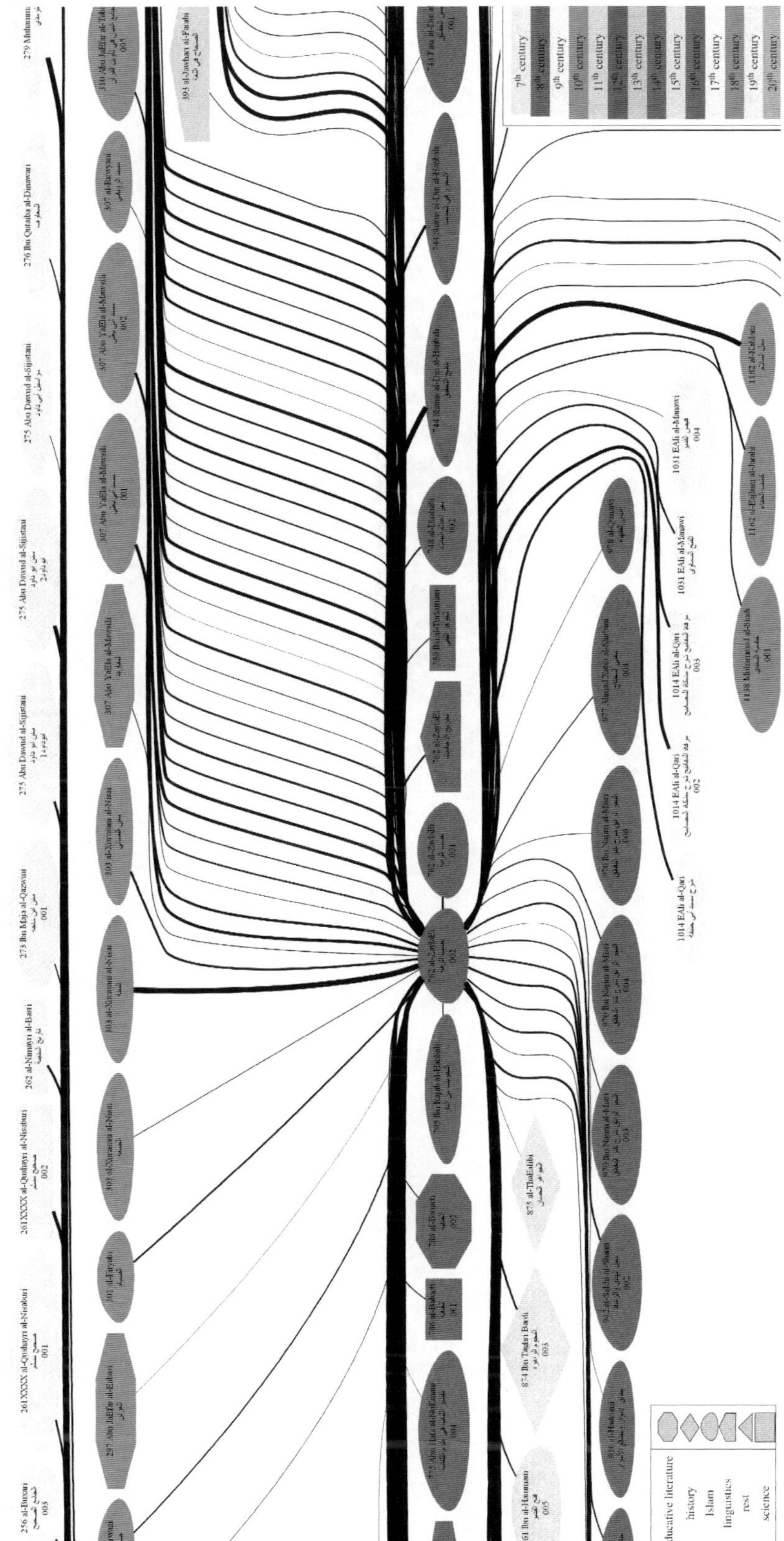

Figure 1: Case study: Zayla'i's Nasab ar-Raya 3 in its context. Parameter $h = 2$. Cut out.

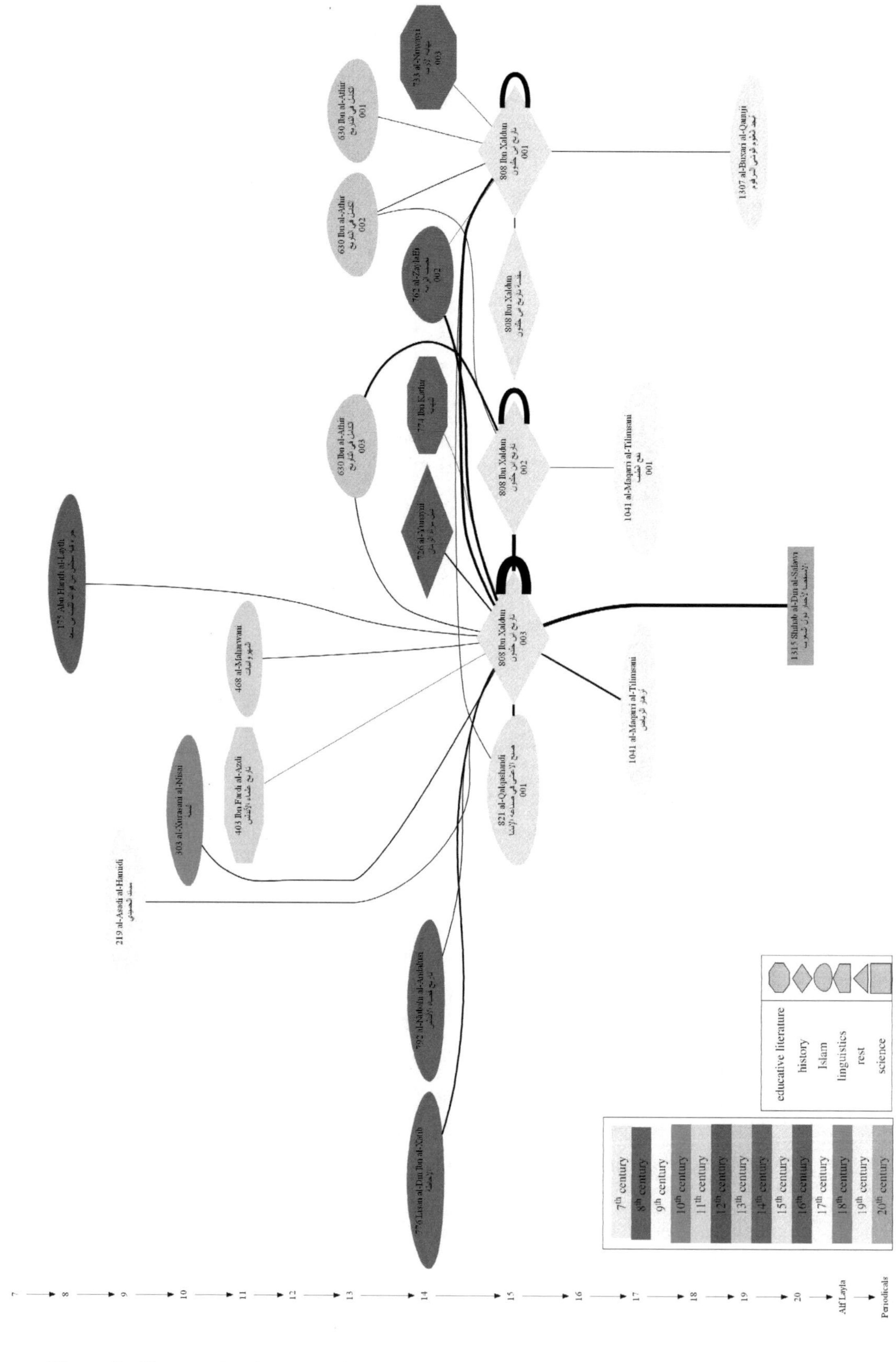

Figure 2: Case study: the network around the Ibn Xaldun's works. Parameter $h = 1.6667$.

Time after Time: Representing Time in Literary Texts

Michael Levison
School of Computing
Queen's University, Canada
levison@cs.queensu.ca

Greg Lessard
French Studies
Queen's University, Canada
greg.lessard@queensu.ca

Abstract

The representation of temporal information in text represents a significant computational challenge. The problem is particularly acute in the case of literary texts, which tend to be massively underspecified, often relying on a network of semantic relations to establish times and timings. This paper shows how a model based on threaded directed acyclic graphs makes it possible to capture a range of subtle temporal information in this type of text and argues for an onomasiological approach which places meaning before form.

1 Time and Text

This paper deals with the representation of temporal phenomena in literary texts. As a result, it builds on work from a number of fields.[1] Thus, it takes as given the longstanding observation from philosophy that time is not a simple issue of days, months and years, but reflects issues of perception and culture (Ricoeur, 1983). At the same time, it assumes that the study of temporal phenomena will be enhanced by use of a formal representation (Allen, 1984). It further assumes the traditional narratological distinction between the information which underlies a text, variously known as the *fabula* or *histoire* and which we will henceforth call the **story** and some particular instantiation of this in text, often called the *sjuzhet* or *récit*, which we will henceforth call the **narrative** (Genette, 1972).

Mani (2010), based on earlier work, suggests that the temporal relations BEFORE, DURING, IMMEDIATELY BEFORE, BEGINS, ENDS, SIMULTANEOUS AND OVERLAPS are adequate for representing time in human languages. This raises the interesting empirical question of how well this model applies to literary texts, given their complex but typically underspecified nature. In fact, in the case of time, a literary text often gives no explicit indication of temporal phenomena, but relies on encyclopedic knowledge available to the reader. In addition, we might ask how different temporal relations are distributed across literary texts, as compared with what is found in expository or other types of texts, or simpler narratives. At the same time, as Lascarides and Asher (1991) point out, it is important to see temporal relations as a subset of a broader range of relations including Narration, Explanation, Background, and Result, all of which have temporal implications.

There does exist a growing body of analyses of narrative texts, but most of these are based on relatively simple third person narratives such as fables. Such texts tend to be event-driven (one thing follows another) and they tend to lack more complex literary phenomena such as first person narrative, where all information is not known, multiple, sometimes competing, perspectives, and significant temporal shifts. It will be important to analyse literary texts in their full complexity before we are capable of pronouncing on the use of time. This will no doubt be aided by research on narrative generation, such as (Callaway and Lester, 2002), (Riedl and Young, 2012), and (Montfort, 2007), where temporal representations at the abstract level are made use of, but this must be complemented by empirical work on actual texts.

The empirical study of temporal relations in complex literary texts will be complicated by the fact that, despite recent progress (for example, Kolomiyets et al. (2012)), parsers still do not match the performance of humans in assigning temporal points and relations. As a result, building a detailed corpus of literary texts will still take some time and much human effort. When it is undertaken, one of the fundamental decisions to be faced will be what is to be represented. Most

[1] In what follows, for lack of space, we restrict ourselves to citing some typical examples from a vast literature.

work to date takes texts themselves as the object of tagging, and schemes such as TimeML (Pustejovsky et al., 2003) are designed to allow quite precise temporal information to be added to texts in the form of markup. As a result, they focus on phenomena in the *narrative* rather than in the *story*. To put this another way, they adopt a *semasiological* perspective (from form to meaning), rather than an *onomasiological* one (from meaning to form) (Baldinger, 1964). However, it is reasonable to ask whether the appropriate level of representation should in fact be one level up, at the level of the story. We argue here that this is the case. Elson (2012) takes a first step in this direction by mapping the textual layer to a propositional layer; however, most of the texts he deals with are relatively simple. We will show below how, in some complex examples, representing temporal phenomena at the story level requires at the least additional 'machinery' based on multiple points of view, temporal shifts including prolepsis, and encyclopedic knowledge, but that it also offers insights into narrative structure not apparent at the textual level.

2 DAGs and Threading

The story which underlies a literary text may be represented by means of a **directed acyclic graph**, henceforth DAG, composed of nodes connected by unidirectional edges. The acyclicity requires that no sequence of edges may return to an earlier node. The nodes carry segments of meaning represented by **semantic expressions**. These are functional representations, described in (Levison et al., 2012). Each semantic expression is composed of elements drawn from a semantic lexicon.

A simple example might be `stab(brutus, caesar)`, where the two entities `brutus` and `caesar` denote certain human beings, and `stab` is a function which takes two entities and returns a completion[2] having the obvious meaning. On the basis of functions such as these, it is possible to construct the DAG shown in Fig. 1.[3]

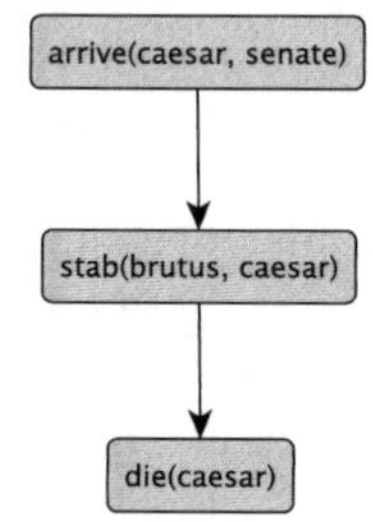

Figure 1: A DAG for the various states of Caesar

The unidirectional edges between the various nodes represent semantic **dependency**, that is, the fact that subsequent nodes depend upon information contained in previous nodes, and by transitive closure, parents of previous nodes. So, in Fig. 1, the expression `stab(brutus, caesar)` depends on the fact that Caesar is at the Senate, while Caesar being dead depends on the stabbing. The relation carried by edges may be one of order (one node occurs before another), or of some sort of causality, whereby a subsequent node is made possible by a previous node. In addition, nodes which convey a coarse level of meaning may themselves be refined into DAGs at a finer level. And so on, recursively.

Since a DAG exists prior to any text which represents it, a text may begin at the start of the DAG and follow the nodes, as in *Caesar arrived at the Senate, then Brutus stabbed him, then he died*, or alternatively at the end, as in *Caesar died because Brutus stabbed him after his arrival at the Senate*, in the middle, as in *Brutus stabbed Caesar after he arrived at the Senate, and then he died*, or even in a zigzag order, as in *Caesar arrived at the Senate and then died because Brutus stabbed him.*[4]

Each of these narrations may be represented by a sequence of nodes, in other words, a thread, showing the order in which the meaning carried by the nodes is presented to the reader. Note that the thread passes through some or all of the nodes, but need not follow the edges of the DAG. Nor is it constrained to be acyclic: it may visit the same node more than once. An example of this is provided by a narration in which the same event is recounted twice. To take an extreme case, in the movie Groundhog Day (`http://www.imdb.com/title/tt0107048/`), the character Phil relives the same day and its events many times.

In our DAGs, we represent threads by a dot-

[2] A completion may be thought of as the semantic equivalent of an utterance, an entity as the semantic equivalent of a noun, and an action as the semantic equivalent of a verb.

[3] The DAGs shown here were constructed with yEd (`http://www.yworks.com/en/products_yed_about.html`), which generates a GraphML representation for each graph. For simplicity, we have ignored representation of tense and aspect in these examples, although the formalism permits this.

[4] For more examples, see (Mani, 2012).

ted line to distinguish them from the edges of the DAG. By threading coarse or refined DAGs, the narration can be at different levels of detail. In addition, a single DAG may be traversed by multiple threads representing, among other things, different points of view. So, for example, suppose that a third party, say Livia, finds Caesar's dead body, observes the stab wounds, and concludes that a previously living Caesar has been killed. From the point of view of the Livia thread, the 'Caesar is dead' node is traversed before the stabbing node (although from Livia's point of view, it may not be clear who has done the stabbing). Alternatively, a fourth character may observe a stabbing in the distance, then on approach note that the stabbee is Caesar, assumed alive until that point, and finally learn that Caesar is dead.

3 Relative and Absolute Timestamps

Within the DAG model, the simple chronological ordering of events or activities requires no extra features except perhaps 'colouring' certain edges to distinguish between those which denote chronological dependence and those whose dependence is based on other reasons. Figure 1 above illustrates this. However, more complex temporal relationships such as 'while' can be signified by nodes indicating relative or absolute times, as in:

```
reltime(7)
   {relative time}
exacttime(0900, 5, Mar, 2013)
   {exact time}
```

Consider, for example, the DAG shown in Fig. 2. Here, both `event1` and `event2` take place after `reltime(7)` and before `reltime(8)`.[5] If no other activities take place in the same context, we might conclude that while `event1` was taking place, `event2` was happening elsewhere. Both events conclude before `event4`. In addition, `event3` occurs after `event1`, but it may have started before or after `reltime(8)`; and there is no information about its relation to `event4`. Additional arguments can be added to specify whether an event is durative or punctual, because nothing says that `event1` actually began at `reltime(7)` and ended at `reltime(8)`. The function `exacttime()` allows us to anchor parts of the DAG at, or more precisely after, specific moments.

[5]The parameters to `reltime`, by the way, are irrelevant; they are included only for the purposes of this commentary.

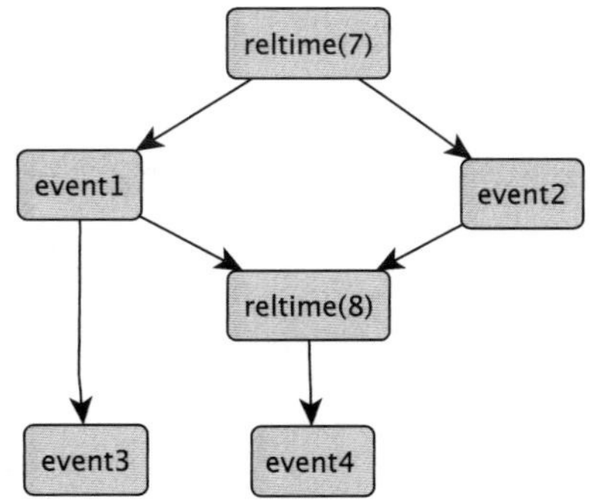

Figure 2: A DAG showing relative times and events

4 Some Empirical Tests of the Formalism

To empirically test the model proposed here, we will examine several actual texts. Of course, these represent only a small selection of a vast range of temporal phenomena. Our object is simply to show how the proposed model may be applied.

4.1 Prolepsis

As noted earlier, a literary text may bring into play a variety of perspectives. One of these is **prolepsis**, or foreknowledge of a future event. Consider the following example from Homer's *Iliad*.[6] Achilles asks Zeus for success in a battle and that Patroclus survive the battle. Zeus grants the first wish, but not the second.[7] As a result, he (Zeus) and by extension, we, as readers, know that Patroclus will die. However Patroclus himself is unaware of this. We may represent this part of the story by means of the DAG shown in Fig. 3, which contains two sets of dependencies, one which links Zeus to the decision that Patroclus will die, and the other which links Patroclus to his fighting and dying. We may then capture the temporality of the narrative by threading this DAG.[8]

An example like this may seem arcane, but cases of multiple points of view, or multiple threading, are found in a variety of textual models. Thus, in a murder mystery, the detective comes to understand the ordering of particular events, including the murder, and may subsequently explain

[6]This instance of prolepsis is discussed in Grethlein (2010).

[7]*Iliad*, ch. 16, v. 249, `http://classics.mit.edu/Homer/iliad.html`.

[8]Threads are shown here by numbered dotted lines to indicate their order, while dependencies are shown by unnumbered solid lines.

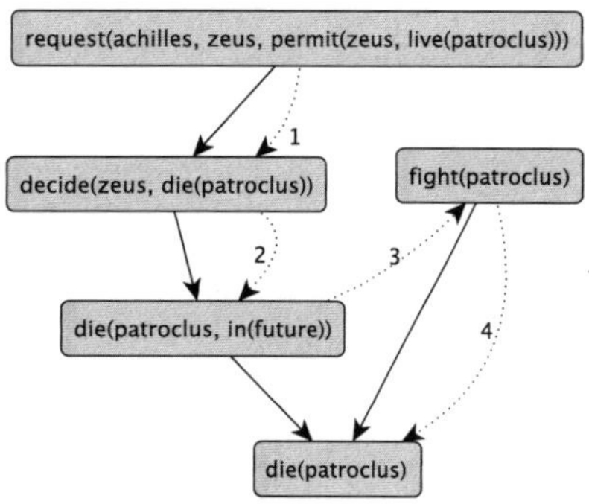

Figure 3: A DAG for part of the *Iliad*

this to the reader.

4.2 Parallel Series of Events

Consider the following passage from the Conan Doyle story entitled *The Red-headed League*.[9]

> When I saw him that afternoon so enwrapped in the music at St. James's Hall ... [10]
>
> "You want to go home, no doubt, Doctor," he remarked as we emerged.
>
> "Yes, it would be as well."
>
> "And I have some business to do which will take some hours. ... to-day being Saturday rather complicates matters. I shall want your help to-night."
>
> "At what time?"
>
> "Ten will be early enough."
>
> "I shall be at Baker Street at ten."
>
> ... It was a quarter-past nine when I started from home and made my way ... to Baker Street. ... On entering his room I found Holmes in animated conversation with two men, ...

The text itself provides two absolute times, one prescriptive, that of the time when Watson is to meet Holmes, and the other descriptive, the time reported by Watson for his leaving home. Another more approximate time is also provided, the fact that Watson and Holmes are listening to music in St James's Hall on a Saturday afternoon. All of these could be marked up in the text itself. However, others would provide a greater challenge. On Watson's return to meet Holmes, he discovers that

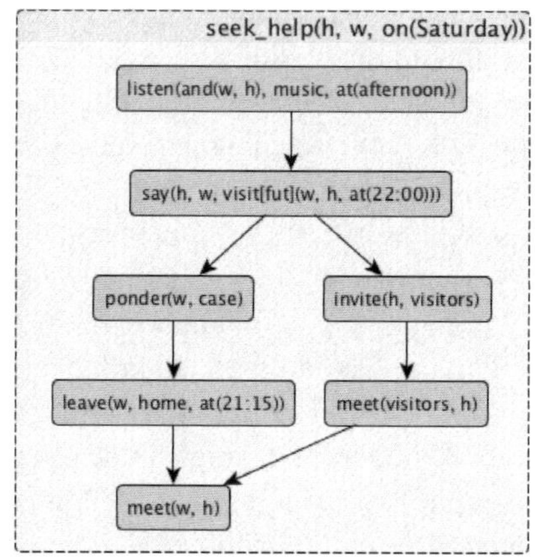

Figure 4: A DAG for part of the *Red-headed League*

others are present, presumably at Holmes' invitation, although this is not specified in the text itself. The chronology of Watson's activities is provided only by its placement in the text, between the conversation with Holmes and the return to meet Holmes, while the arrival of the others cannot be marked up at all at the textual level since it is not even mentioned in the text. Such a model provides a serious challenge to a semasiological markup, for obvious reasons. However, it may be easily represented by a DAG, as shown in Fig. 4.

Note that the nodes of the DAG are all enclosed in a higher-level node situated on Saturday. This 'envelope' provides the framework for the detailed events. However, within this envelope, a branching occurs, separating Watson's explicitly noted activities from those which we must suppose Holmes to have accomplished. The two series are bracketed between a relative temporal marker (the moment when Watson and Holmes leave each other) and an absolute temporal marker (Watson's arrival at Holmes' lodgings around 10).

4.3 Access to Encyclopaedic Information

Reading a text is not a simple activity. Among other things, it requires a constant reference to background 'encyclopaedic' information. The nature of this information will vary from reader to reader. As an illustration, consider the following paragraph, which opens Flaubert's novel *Salammbô*.[11]

[9]First published in the *Strand* magazine in 1891. See http://www.gutenberg.org/ebooks/1661.

[10]Several non-pertinent elements of the text have been elided. These are shown by suspension points.

[11]We provide here the English translation from http://www.gutenberg.org/files/1290/1290-h/1290-h.htm#link2HCH0001.

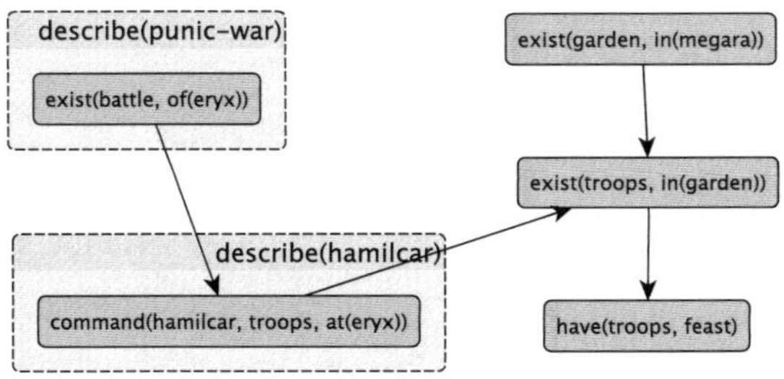

Figure 5: A DAG for the introduction to *Salammbô*

> It was at Megara, a suburb of Carthage, in the gardens of Hamilcar. The soldiers whom he had commanded in Sicily were having a great feast to celebrate the anniversary of the battle of Eryx, and as the master was away, and they were numerous, they ate and drank with perfect freedom.

At the most basic level, any reader may use the tense (*had commanded*) and some lexical items (*anniversary*) to determine the anteriority of the battle of Eryx with respect to the feast. However, more educated readers will probably be able to use the proper name *Carthage* to locate the text in the far past, while even more educated readers will be able to use the names *Hamilcar* and *Eryx* to place the feast after the period 244-242 BCE.

We may represent the interplay between what is given by the text and the information available to the reader (which, importantly, is also representable by a DAG) as shown in Fig. 5, where we see that the node `exist(troops...)`, represented in the text, depends on the node `command(hamilcar...)` also represented in the text. However, this latter node is a subnode of the higher-level node `describe(hamilcar)`, which provides information (including temporal information) not present in the text. Similarly, the node `exist(battle...)`, present in the text, is part of another higher-level node (`describe(punic-war)`), which contains more detailed encyclopaedic information.

This model captures both the temporal elasticity provided by the interplay of logical dependency and the varying levels of temporal assignment noted above. To put this another way, it captures the set of readings which the same text may carry for different readers. In particular, different readings may thread this DAG at different levels of granularity, some coarse, some finer.

5 Conclusions and Next Steps

Although they are limited to issues of time, the examples studied above suggest that an onomasiological approach gives access to textual and literary phenomena which escape tagging of textual contents alone. While the use of DAGs and threading currently requires human intervention, the output of the model, by its formality, provides a means of studying in detail the instantiation of stories as narratives, and thereby, a complement to existing approaches to literary time.

References

James F. Allen. 1984. Towards a general theory of action and time. *Artificial Intelligence*, 23:123–154.

Kurt Baldinger. 1964. Sémasiologie et onomasiologie. *Revue de linguistique romane*, 28:249–272.

Charles Callaway and James Lester. 2002. Narrative prose generation. *Artificial Intelligence*, 139(2):213–252.

David K. Elson. 2012. *Modeling Narrative Discourse*. PhD thesis, Columbia University.

Gérard Genette. 1972. *Figures III*. Éditions du Seuil, Paris.

Jonas Grethlein. 2010. The narrative reconfiguration of time beyond Ricoeur. *Poetics Today*, 31(2):313–329.

Oleksandr Kolomiyets, Steven Bethard and Marie-France Moens. 2012. Extracting narrative timelines as temporal dependency structures. In *Proceedings of the 50th Annual Meeting of the Association for Computational Linguistics (ACL'2012)*, pp. 88-97.

Alex Lascarides and Nicholas Asher. 1991. Discourse relations and defeasible knowledge. In *Proceedings of the 29th Annual Meeting of the Association of Computational Linguistics (ACL91)*, pp. 55-63.

Michael Levison, Greg Lessard, Craig Thomas, and Matthew Donald. 2012. *The Semantic Representation of Natural Language*. Bloomsbury Publishing, London.

Inderjeet Mani. 2012. *Computational Modeling of Narrative*. Morgan and Claypool, San Rafael, CA.

Inderjeet Mani. 2010. *The Imagined Moment: Time, Narrative and Computation*. University of Nebraska Press, Lincoln, Nebraska.

Nick Montfort. 2007. Ordering events in interactive fiction narratives. In *Proceedings of the AAAI Fall Symposium on Interactive Narrative Technologies.* Technical Report FS-07-05, B.S. Magerki and M. Riedl, eds., AAAI Press, Menlo Park, CA, pp. 87–94.

James Pustejovsky, Jose M. Castaño, Robert Ingria, Roser Saurí, Robert Gaizauskas, Andrea Setzer, and Graham Katz. 2003. TimeML: Robust specification of event and temporal expressions in text. In *Fifth International Workshop on Computational Semantics (IWCS-5).*

Paul Ricœur. 1983. *Temps et récit.* Volume 1. Éditions du Seuil, Paris.

Mark Riedl and R. Michael Young. 2010. Narrative planning: balancing plot and character. *Journal of Artificial Intelligence Research*, 39:217–268.

Structure-based Clustering of Novels

Mariona Coll Ardanuy
Trier University
ardanuy@uni-trier.de

Caroline Sporleder
Trier University
sporledc@uni-trier.de

Abstract

To date, document clustering by genres or authors has been performed mostly by means of stylometric and content features. With the premise that novels are societies in miniature, we build social networks from novels as a strategy to quantify their plot and structure. From each social network, we extract a vector of features which characterizes the novel. We perform clustering over the vectors obtained, and the resulting groups are contrasted in terms of author and genre.

1 Introduction

In recent years, the interest for quantitative methods of literary analysis has grown significantly. Humanities scholars and researchers are increasingly aware of the potential of data-driven approaches in a field that has traditionally been studied from a 'close reading' perspective. Large repositories of literary text together with the development of promising techniques from fields such as text mining or information extraction offer advantages that open new possibilities to the field of literature studies.

So far, most quantitative studies of literature have focused mainly on form and content. Structure and plot, considered key dimensions in a novel, have often been ignored due to the complexity in quantifying them. In this study, we explore the contribution of features that are directly related to them. With this goal, we represent a novel as a social network of characters (a technique that is not novel in the field of quantitative literary analysis), from which to extract features that can be used to perform document clustering. The outcome of the clustering will be a grouping of novels according to their structural similarity.

This is an exploratory study to determine to what degree the structure and plot of a novel are representative of the genre to which it belongs and characteristic of the style of its author. Two hypotheses are made on the basis of this premise. The first is that the structure and plot of the novel represented as a static and dynamic social network is key to predict the literary genre to which a novel belongs. The second is that the inner structure of the society depicted by the author in a novel is representative of this author. This approach introduces the use of automatically extracted static and dynamic networks to perform large-scale analyses of novels, by representing them as vectors of features that can then be used to compare the novels in terms of genre and authorship.

The rest of this paper is organized as follows. In Section 2 we present the related work. Section 3 describes the method employed in turning a novel into the vector of features chosen to characterize it. The experiments conducted are discussed in Section 4 and the results and analysis of them in Section 5. We discuss the results in Section 6 and conclude in Section 7.

2 Related Work

2.1 Unsupervised Document Classification

Unsupervised document classification (or 'document clustering') consists in automatically grouping a set of documents based on the similarities among them. Unlike its supervised counterpart, it does not require neither labeled training data nor prior knowledge of the classes into which the texts are to be categorized. Instead, documents—represented as vectors of features—that are similar are grouped together, yielding a clustering that is dependent on the features chosen to characterize the document. Due to the lack of supervision, it is not guaranteed that the resulting clustering corresponds to the classes in which we are interested (Zhang, 2013).

Unsupervised authorship analysis from documents is the task of automatically grouping texts that share the same author, by determining the set of features that distinguish one author from any other. The first approaches focused mainly on stylometrics (Ledger and Merriam (1994), Holmes and Forsyth (1995), Baayen et al. (1996), and Aaronson (2001)). More recent approaches use content-based features, such as Akiva and Koppel (2012) and Layton et al. (2011). Pavlyshenko (2012) brings document clustering by author to the literature domain. The lexicon of the author is in this work represented as semantic fields (the author's idiolect) on which Singular Value Decomposition is applied.

Much less effort has been devoted to the task of clustering documents by the genre in which they fall. Examples of this are Gupta et al. (2005), Poudat and Cleuziou (2003), and Bekkerman et al. (2007). The work of Allison et al. (2011) uses stylometric features to cluster 36 novels according to genre. The resulting clustering is only partially successful, but made its authors realize that the classification was not only obeying to genre criteria, but also to authorship. The stylistic signature of every document corresponded to a strong 'author' signal, rather than to the 'genre' signal.

2.2 Literary Quantitative Analysis

The reviewed approaches have in common that they use stylometric or content-based features. However, a novel should not be reduced to the dimensions of punctuation, morphology, syntax and semantics. This literary form has a depth, a complex structure of plot, characters and narration. The plot of a novel is defined in the Russian structuralism school by the collection of its characters and the actions they carry out (Bakhtin (1941), Propp (1968)). It could be said that every novel is a society in miniature.[1] Moretti (2011), concerned about how plot can be quantified, explores extensively the impact characters have on it. To this end, Moretti represents the characters of William Shakespeare's *Hamlet* as a social network. Several experiments (removing the protagonist, isolates, or a connecting character from the network) show how the plot changes accordingly to the alteration in the structure of characters. Sack (2012) proposes using social networks of characters as a mechanism for generating plots artificially.

One of the first attempts of combining social networks and literature was in Alberich et al. (2002). They built a social network from the Marvel comics in which characters are the nodes, linked by their co-occurrence in the same book. The authors note that the resulting network was very similar to a real social network. In Newman and Girvan (2003), the authors used a hand-built social network with the main characters of Victor Hugo's *Les Misérables* to detect communities of characters that were densely connected. These communities, in the words of the authors, "clearly reflect[ed] the subplot structure of the book".

Elson et al. (2010) introduced an interesting idea: so far, two characters had always been linked by an edge if they occurred in the same text-window. In their approach, characters are linked if they converse. The networks are built in an automatic fashion, and heuristics are used to cluster co-referents. The authors's analysis of the networks debunks long standing literary hypotheses. Celikyilmaz et al. (2010) extracts dialogue interactions in order to analyze semantic orientations of social networks from literature. In order to perform large-scale analyses of the works, both Rydberg-Cox (2011) and Suen et al. (2013) extract networks from structured text: Greek tragedies the first, plays and movie scripts the latter.

All the approaches mentioned above produce static networks which are flat representations of the novel as a whole. In them, past, present, and future are represented at once. By means of static networks, time turns into space. The recent work by Agarwal et al. (2012) questions the validity of static network analysis. Their authors introduce the concept of dynamic network analysis for literature, motivated by the idea that static networks can distort the importance of the characters (exemplified through an analysis of Lewis Carroll's *Alice in Wonderland*). A dynamic social network is but the collection of independent networks for each of the parts in which the novel is divided.

3 Turning Novels into Social Networks

3.1 Human Name Recognition

A social network is a structure that captures the relations between a set of actors. The actors in a novel are its characters, and thus extracting person names from the raw text is necessarily the first step

[1]This is particularly evident in William M. Thackeray's novel *Vanity Fair* through the ironic and mocking voice of the narrator, making the reader aware of his describing much more than just the adventures and missfortunes of a collection of invented characters.

to construct a social network from a novel. To that end, we used the `Stanford Named Entity Recognizer` (Stanford NER)[2], to which we applied post-processing recognition patterns in order to enhance its performance in the literary domain.[3] Stanford NER tags the entities on a per-token basis. The name 'Leicester' might be tagged as `person` in one paragraph and as `location` in the next one. With the assumption that a novel is a small universe in which one proper name is likely to refer to the same entity throughout the novel, we eliminate these inconsistencies by re-tagging the file, so that each entity recognized during the filtering is tagged as `person` throughout the file. Each proper name that has been tagged as a `person` more times than as a `location` is also re-tagged consistently as `person`.

Table 1 shows the evaluation of the person name recognizer in novels both originally in English and translated, both before (`StanfordNER`) and after (`FilteredNER`) the filtering. The filtering improves the performance of the entity recognizer significantly in the case of English literature, and only slightly in foreign literature. We evaluated eight chapters randomly picked from eight different novels.[4]

	Precision	*Recall*	F_1*Score*
StanfordNER-Eng	0.9684	0.8101	0.8822
FilteredNER-Trn	0.9816	0.9970	0.9892
StanfordNER-Eng	0.9287	0.7587	0.8351
FilteredNER-Trn	0.8589	0.8277	0.8430

Table 1: Evaluation of person recognition.

3.2 Character Resolution

A list of person names is not a list of characters. Among the extracted names are 'Miss Lizzy', 'Miss Elizabeth', 'Miss Elizabeth Bennet', 'Lizzy', 'Miss Eliza Bennet', 'Elizabeth Bennet', and 'Elizabeth', all of them names corresponding to one only character, the protagonist of Jane Austen's *Pride and Prejudice*. A social network relates entities, and thus it is a crucial step to group all the co-referents together. The task of character resolution has been done in three steps:

- *Human name parsing.* We used an extended version of the Python module `python-nameparser`[5] to parse the recognized names into its different components, so that a name like 'Mr. Sherlock Homes', would have 'Mr.' tagged as *title*, 'Sherlock' as *first name* and 'Holmes' as *last name*.

- *Gender assignation.* Each human name is assigned a gender (*male*, *female*, or *unknown*). We have four lists: with typical male titles ('Sir', 'Lord', etc.), with female titles ('Miss', 'Lady', etc.), with 2579 male first names[6] and with 4636 female first names[7]. To assign a gender to a human name, first the title is considered. If the title is empty or non-informative, the first name is considered. If none are informative of the gender of the character, immediate context is considered: a counter keeps track of counts of 'his' and 'himself' (on the one hand), and of 'her' and 'herself' (on the other) appearing in a window of at most 3 words to the right of the name. Depending on which of the two counters is higher, the human name is assigned one gender or the other. If the conditions are not met, the gender remains unknown.

- *Matching algorithm.* A matching algorithm is responsible for grouping the different co-referents of the same entity from less to more ambiguous:

  1. Names with `title`, `first name` and `last name` (e.g. 'Miss Elizabeth Bennet').
  2. Names with `first name` and `last name` (e.g. 'Elizabeth Bennet').
  3. Names with `title` and `first name` (e.g. 'Miss Elizabeth').
  4. Names with `title` and `last name` (e.g. 'Miss Bennet').
  5. Names with only `first name` or `last name` (e.g. 'Elizabeth' or 'Bennet').

For each matching step, three points are considered: a first name can appear as a nick-

[2] `http://nlp.stanford.edu/software/CRF-NER.shtml`

[3] A list of 178 honorifics such as 'Sir', 'Lady', or 'Professor' indicating that the adherent proper name is a person, and a list of 83 verbs of utterance such as 'say', 'complain' or 'discuss' in both present and past forms indicating the immediate presence of a person.

[4] *Little Dorrit* and *The Pickwick Papers* by Charles Dickens, *Pride and Prejudice* from Jane Austen, *Dr. Jekyll and Mr. Hyde* by R. L. Stevenson, *The Hunchback of Notre-Dame* by Victor Hugo, *The Phantom of the Opera* by Gaston Leroux, *War and Peace* by Leo Tolstoy, and *Don Quixote of La Mancha* by Miguel de Cervantes.

[5] `http://code.google.com/p/python-nameparser/`

[6] Source: `http://www.cs.cmu.edu/Groups/AI/areas/nlp/corpora/names/male.txt`

[7] Source: `http://www.cs.cmu.edu/Groups/AI/areas/nlp/corpora/names/female.txt`

name ('Lizzy' is 'Elizabeth')[8], a first name can appear as an initial ('J. Jarndyce' is 'John Jarndyce'), and the genders of the names to match must agree ('Miss Sedley' matches 'Amelia Sedley', but not 'Jos Sedley'). If after these steps a referent is still ambiguous, it goes to its most common match (e.g. 'Mr. Holmes' might refer both to 'Sherlock Holmes' and to his brother 'Mycroft Holmes'. According to our algorithm, 'Mr. Holmes' matches both names, so we assume that it refers to the most relevant character of the novel, in this case the protagonist, 'Sherlock Holmes'.

Evaluating character resolution is not a simple task, since the impact of a misidentification will depend on the relevance of the wrongly identified character. The evaluation that we propose (see Table 2) for this task takes into consideration only the 10 most relevant characters in 10 novels.[9]

	Precision	*Recall*	F_1*Score*
EnglishLit	0.9866	0.9371	0.9612
ForeignLit	0.9852	0.9086	0.9454

Table 2: Evaluation of character resolution.

The evaluation of the gender assignment task (see Table 3) is done on the total number of characters from six different novels.[10]

	Precision	*Recall*	F_1*Score*
EnglishLit	0.9725	0.8676	0.9171
ForeignLit	0.9603	0.5734	0.7175

Table 3: Evaluation of gender assignment.

3.3 Network Construction

As mentioned in Section 2, two main approaches to create character networks from literary fiction have been proposed. In the first one (hereafter **conversational network**), nodes (i.e. characters) are related by means of an edge if there is a spoken interaction between them. In the second approach (hereafter **co-occurrence network**), nodes are linked whenever they co-occur in the same window of text. A conversational network is well-suited to represent plays, where social interaction is almost only represented by means of dialogue. However, much of the interaction in novels is done off-dialogue through the description of the narrator or indirect interactions. Thus, using a conversational network might not suffice to capture all interactions, and it would definitely have severe limitations in novels with unmarked dialogue, little dialogue or none.[11]

The networks built in this approach are static and dynamic co-occurrence networks.[12] A **static network** allows better visualization of the novel as a whole, and the features extracted from it correspond to a time agnostic analysis of the novel's plot. A **dynamic network** is a sequence of subnetworks, each of which constructed for each of the chapters into which the novel is divided. In it, one can visualize the development of the characters throughout the novel. In both networks, nodes are linked if they co-occur in the same window of text, which in our case is set to be a paragraph, a natural division of text according to discourse. The graph is **undirected** (the direction of the interaction is ignored) and **weighted** (the weight is the number of interactions between the two linked nodes). In 1st person novels, the off-dialogue occurrences of pronoun "I" are added to the node of the character who narrates the story, in order to avoid the narrator (probably the protagonist of the novel) to be pushed to the background.

We used the python library `Networkx`[13] to construct the networks and the network analysis software `Gephi`[14] to visualize them.

[8] A list of names and their hypocoristics is used to deal with this. Source: `https://metacpan.org/source/BRIANL/Lingua-EN-Nickname-1.14/nicknames.txt`

[9] *The Mystery of Edwin Drood* and *Oliver Twist* by Charles Dickens, *Sense and Sensibility* by Jane Austen, *Vanity Fair* by William M. Thackeray, *The Hound of the Baskervilles* by Arthur Conan Doyle, *Around the World in Eighty Days* by Jules Verne, *The Phantom of the Opera* by Gaston Leroux, *Les Misérables* by Victor Hugo, *The Three Musketeers* by Alexandre Dumas, and *Madame Bovary* by Gustave Flaubert.

[10] *Oliver Twist* by Charles Dickens, *Sense and Sensibility* by Jane Austen, *The Hound of the Baskervilles* by Arthur Conan Doyle, *Around the World in Eighty Days* by Jules Verne, *The Phantom of the Opera* by Gaston Leroux, *On the Eve* by Ivan Turgenev.

[11] Examples are Cormac McCarthy's *On the road*, George Orwell's *Nineteen Eighty-Four*, and Margaret Yourcenar's *Memoirs of Hadrian*.

[12] In section 3.4, we offer a qualitative analysis of some networks. We have already motivated our choice for using co-occurrence networks instead of conversational. Both methods would yield very different networks. The reason why we do not provide compared results between both approaches is that we do not consider them quantitatively comparable, since they represent and capture different definitions of what a social relation is.

[13] `http://networkx.github.io/`

[14] `http://gephi.org/`

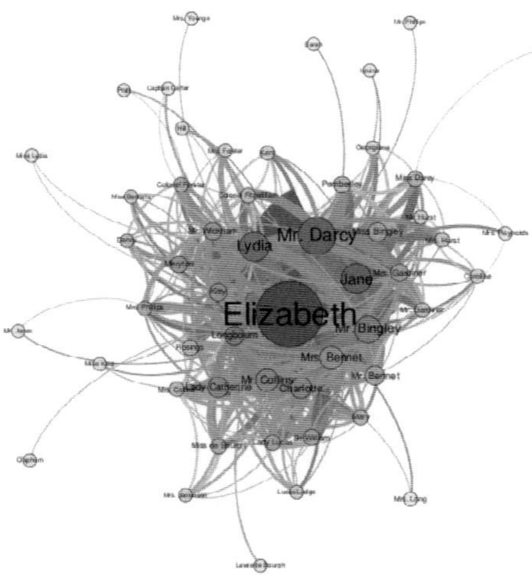

Figure 1: Static network of *Pride and Prejudice*.

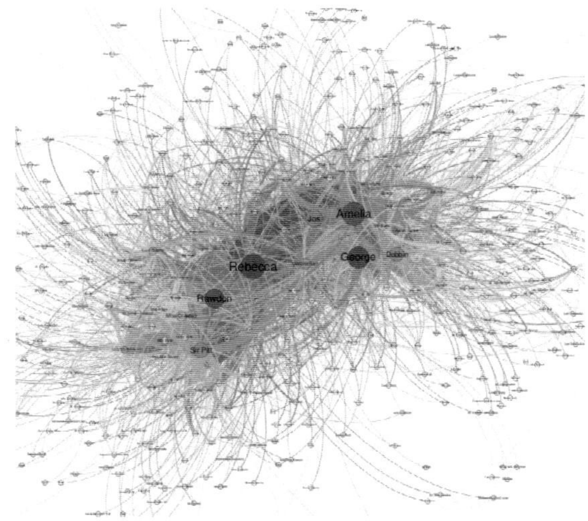

Figure 2: Static network of *Vanity Fair*.

3.4 Network Analysis

The aim of extracting social networks from novels is to turn a complex object (the novel) into a schematic representation of the core structure of the novel. Figures 1 and 2 are two examples of static networks, corresponding to Jane Austen's *Pride and Prejudice* and William M. Thackeray's *Vanity Fair* respectively. Just a glimpse to the network is enough to make us realize that they are very different in terms of structure.

Pride and Prejudice has an indisputable main character (Elizabeth) and the whole network is organized around her. The society depicted in the novel is that of the heroine. *Pride and Prejudice* is the archetypal romantic comedy and is also often considered a Bildungsroman.

The community represented in ***Vanity Fair*** could hardly be more different. Here the novel does not turn around one only character. Instead, the protagonism is now shared by at least two nodes, even though other very centric foci can be seen. The network is spread all around these characters. The number of minor characters and isolate nodes is in comparison huge. *Vanity Fair* is a satirical novel with many elements of social criticism.

Static networks show the skeleton of novels, dynamic networks its development, by incorporating a key dimension of the novel: time, represented as a succession of chapters. In the time axis, characters appear, disappear, evolve. In a dynamic network of Jules Verne's ***Around the World in Eighty Days***, we would see that the character Aouda appears for the first time in chapter 13. From that moment on, she is Mr. Fogg's companion for the rest of the journey and the reader's companion for the rest of the book. This information is lost in a static network, in which the group of very static gentlemen of a London club are sitting very close from a consul in Suez, a judge in Calcutta, and a captain in his transatlantic boat. All these characters would never co-occur (other than by mentions) in a dynamic network.

4 Experiments

At the beginning of this paper we ask ourselves whether the plot of a novel (here represented as its structure of characters) can be used to identify literary genres or to determine its author. We propose two main experiments to investigate the role of the novel structure in the identification of an author and of a genre. Both experiments are considered as an unsupervised classification task.

4.1 Document Clustering by Genre

Data collection.[15] This study does not have a quantified, analogous experiment with which to compare the outcome. Thus, our approach has required constructing a corpus of novels from scratch and building an appropriate baseline. We have collected a representative sample of the most influential novels of the Western world. The resulting dataset contains 238 novels[16]. Each novel

[15]The complete list of works and features used for both experiments can be found in `http://www.coli.uni-saarland.de/~csporled/SocialNetworksInNovels.html`.

[16]Source: `http://www.gutenberg.org/`

was annotated with the genre to which it belongs. The task of assigning a genre to a novel is not trivial. The Russian literary critic Mikhail Bakhtin relates the inherent difficulties in the study of the novelistic genre, being the novel the "sole genre that continues to develop, that is as yet uncompleted" (Bakhtin, 1981). Different sources differ in categorizing the same novels, some novels are labeled with more than one genre, and even some novels are not categorized at all. The process of building and labeling the corpus has therefore been long and laborious.

The decision on how many genres there should be was taken based on observation, resulting in **11 most seen genres**: adventure, historical, romance, satirical, gothic, Bildungsroman, picaresque, mystery, social criticism, science fiction, and children fiction. In order to annotate the data, different sources were contrasted, among which the study guides from Spark Notes[17] and Shmoop[18], popular reading web portals such as Goodread[19], the Wikipedia[20], and different literary research studies for each particular novel. Each novel has been annotated with a maximum of three genres in those cases in which sources did not agree.

Experimental Setup. We propose four different set-ups, representing different fractions of the data set. The **enCorpus** is the set of 184 novels originally written in English. The **trCorpus** is the set of 54 novels originally not written in English, in their translated version. The **alCorpus** is the whole dataset, 238 novels. The **19Corpus** is a subset of 118 British novels from the 19th Century.

4.2 Document Clustering by Author

Data collection. The evaluation of document clustering by author does not pose nearly as many challenges. For this experiment, we have disregarded 1st person narratives.[21] We collected 45 novels from 7 different authors: five British authors from the 19th Century (Jane Austen (*6 novels*), Charles Dickens (*11*), Elizabeth Gaskell (*5*), George Eliot (*7*), and William Thackeray (*6*)), and two Russian realism authors (Ivan Turgenev (*6*) and Fyodor Dostoyevsky (*4*)). For investigative reasons, we have also included the seven novels from the *Harry Potter* fantasy series, by the contemporary British author J. K. Rowling.

Experimental Setup. We propose four different set-ups, focusing on the author. Table 4 shows the authors included in each experiment.

#Corpus	Authors
Corpus1	Austen, Dickens, Thackeray, Eliot, Gaskell
Corpus2	Austen, Dickens, Thackeray, Eliot, Gaskell, Dostoyevsky, Turgenev
Corpus3	Austen, Dickens, Thackeray, Eliot, Gaskell, Rowling
Corpus4	Austen, Dickens, Thackeray, Eliot, Gaskell, Dostoyevsky, Turgenev, Rowling

Table 4: Authors in each corpus fraction.

4.3 Feature Selection

The static features that we have used for clustering are mostly well-known metrics drawn from social network analysis. These include measures such as graph density, average clustering coefficient, diameter, radius, proportion of eccentric, central and isolate nodes, and relevance of the main node. Variations of social network analysis metrics are: proportion of male characters, relative weight of the main node, relative weight of the second biggest node, of the ten most important nodes, and of the isolate nodes, and proportion of edges of the main character. Dynamic features control the continued presence of the protagonist throughout the novel, the varying proportion of characters in each stage of the novel, and proportion of characters appearing in only one stage.

In the clustering experiment by genre, we differenciate between features that apply to 1st and 3rd person point-of-view to avoid the disproportionate weight of the narrator to incline the results. Some features not used in the author experiment are added, such as the absolute size of the network both in terms of nodes and of length of the novel, the presence of the main character in the title of the book, the point-of-view, the number of chapters and whether the narrator is known. The author experiment has a total of 27 features, while the genre experiment has 55[22]. The **baseline** we propose is based on content: for each novel a vector with a raw Bag-of-words representation is generated.

For the clustering, we use the `Weka EM` implementation, in which the number of clusters was al-

[17] `http://www.sparknotes.com/`

[18] `http://www.shmoop.com/literature/`

[19] `http://www.goodreads.com/`

[20] `http://www.wikipedia.org`

[21] Whereas the point of view in which the story is written might be indicative of a genre (e.g. some genres might be more prone to use 1st person), in most cases it is not of an author, since they are many the authors that equally use different points of view in their novels.

[22] See footnote 15.

ready pre-defined to the desired number of classes (11 in the case of clustering by genre, 5-8 in the case of clustering by author).

5 Results and Analysis

The results of the clustering are evaluated with respect to the annotated data. The task of evaluating the results of a clustering is not trivial, since one cannot know with certainty which labels correspond to which clusters. In this approach, the labelling of the classes relies on `Weka`'s[23](Hall et al., 2009) **Classes to clusters** evaluation functionality, which assigns a label to the cluster which contains most of the elements of the labeled class, as long as the class is not defining another cluster. The evaluation is based on three popular metrics: purity, entropy and F_1 measure. In the clustering experiments by genre, if one novel is classified as at least one of the correct classes, we consider it to be correct.

#Corpus	**Baseline**			**Our approach**		
Metric	Pur	Ent	F_1S	Pur	Ent	F_1S
`enCorpus`	0.45	0.34	0.31	0.46	0.34	**0.33**
`trCorpus`	0.56	0.28	**0.34**	0.44	0.31	0.27
`alCorpus`	0.42	0.35	**0.27**	0.40	0.36	0.26
`19Corpus`	0.53	0.29	0.34	0.58	0.29	**0.40**

Table 5: Genre clustering evaluation.

Table 5 shows the results of both the baseline and our approach in the clustering task by genre.[24] The clustering results are negative, even though not random. The performance is slightly better in works originally written in English (`enCorpus` and `19Corpus`). The reason why the `19Corpus` performs significantly better than the rest of the collections is probably to be found in the fact that all other collections contain documents from very different ages (up to five centuries of difference) and countries of origin. Since novels usually depict the society of the moment, it is not surprising that the more local the collection of texts, the higher the performance of the approach is.

As can be seen in Table 6, the performance of both the baseline and our approach in clustering by author is much higher than by genre.[25] The performance of the baseline approach decreases as

#Corpus	**Baseline**			**Our approach**		
Metric	Pur	Ent	F_1S	Pur	Ent	F_1S
`Corpus1`	0.74	0.20	**0.74**	0.63	0.26	0.63
`Corpus2`	0.64	0.23	0.55	0.60	0.28	**0.60**
`Corpus3`	0.74	0.19	**0.71**	0.71	0.22	**0.71**
`Corpus4`	0.58	0.25	0.52	0.62	0.24	**0.60**

Table 6: Author clustering evaluation.

it goes away from the same period and same origin, but also as the number of authors in which to cluster the novels increases. Our approach does not suffer too much from the increasing number of classes in which to cluster. Interesting enough, we see how the baseline and our approach yield similar results in both clustering tasks even if the features could not be more different from one vector to the other. As future work, we plan to combine both methods in order to enhance the results.

6 Discussion

6.1 Clustering by Genre

Genres are not clear and distinct classes. By observing the 'incorrectly labeled' cases from our network-based method, we find some interesting patterns: some genres tend to be misclassified always into the same "incorrect" genre. It is the case, for example, of the categories *Bildungsroman* and *picaresque*. Some novels that should have been labeled Bildungsroman are instead considered picaresque, or vice versa. Indeed, one can easily find certain characteristics that are shared in both genres, such as a strong protagonist and a whole constellation of minor characters around him or her. What distinguishes them from being the same genre is that the focus and goal in a Bildungsroman is on the development of the main character. Picaresque novels, on the contrary, usually have no designed goal for the protagonist, and consist of a sequence of adventures, most of them unrelated and inconsequential to each other. The same kind of strong relationship exists, in a lesser extent, between *historical*, *social* and *satirical* genres. These three genres are somewhat intertwined. Social criticism might be carried out through a satirical novel, which might be set to take place in the past, making it a historical novel. Our method classifies these three genres indistinctly together, and this might well be because of their very similar structural characteristics.

We consider this experiment a first step in the task of novel clustering by genre. The method that

[23] `http://www.cs.waikato.ac.nz/ml/index.html`

[24] The yielded clusters and their quality can be found in `http://www.coli.uni-saarland.de/~csporled/SocialNetworksInNovels.html`

[25] See footnote 24.

we have presented is far from being perfected. We have used all the features that we have designed in an unweighted way and without optimizing them. However, it is assumed that some features will have a bigger impact than others at determining genres. A blunt analysis of the role of the features informs that the relevance of the protagonist node is key, for example, to identify genres such as Bildungsroman and picaresque. A high proportion of minor or isolate nodes is, for example, a very good indicator of satirical, social, and historical genres. An unknown narrator is a good indicator that we are in front of a science fiction novel, while a mixed point of view is usually kept for either science fiction, gothic, or mystery novels.

6.2 Clustering by Author

The clustering by author is much clearer than the clustering by genre, and very interesting patterns can be found when looked in detail. One can learn, for instance, that the structure of Jane Austen novels are in the antipodes of the structure of William M. Thackeray's works (as could be inferred from Figures 1 and 2). These two authors are, alongside Rowling, the easiest authors to identify. In fact, a clustering of only the novels by these three authors result in a perfectly clear-cut grouping with no misclassifications. Dickens and Eliot are on the other hand the most difficult authors to identify, partly because their structures are more varied.

An in-depth study of the role of each feature in the clustering provides a very interesting view of the literary work of each author. We can see in our sample that female writers (in particular Austen and Gaskell) have a much higher proportion of female characters than male writers (in particular Dickens, Turgenev, and Dostoyevsky), with Thackeray and Rowling depicting a more equal society. Examples of behaviors that can be read from the clustering are many. The very low graph density of Thackeray's novels contrasts with the high density of the novels by Austen and Turgenev, whereas all of Gaskell's novels have a strikingly similar graph density. In the case of the *Harry Potter* books, the first ones are significantly denser than the last ones. The role of the protagonist also varies depending on the author. It is very important in the works by Austen, Gaskell, and Rowling, in which the presence of the protagonist is constant throughout the novel. Turgenev's protagonists are also very strong, even though their presence varies along the chapters. Thackeray, on the other hand, is by far the author that gives more weight to minor characters and isolates. Turgenev has a high proportion of isolate nodes, while they are almost null in works by Rowling and Austen. The dynamic features show the different distributions of characters over the time of the novel. They allow us see very clearly in which stages coincide the maximum number of characters (the falling action in the case of Austen, the dénouement in the case of Eliot, the rising action in the case of Rowling). They allow us to see also how a very high proportion of characters in Thackeray's novels appear in only one stage in the novel, to then disappear. In the other side of the spectrum are Austen and Dostoyevsky, whose characters arrive in the novel to stay. These are only some of the most evident conclusions that can be drawn from the author-clustering experiment. A more in-depth analysis could be useful, for example, to identify changes in the work of one same author.

7 Conclusion

This work is a contribution to the field of quantitative literary analysis. We have presented a method to build static and dynamic social networks from novels as a way of representing structure and plot. Our goal was two-fold: to learn which role the structure of a novel plays in identifying a novelistic genre, and to understand to what extent the structure of the novel is a fingerprint of the style of the author. We have designed two experiments shaped as unsupervised document classification tasks. The first experiment, clustering by genre resulted in a negative clustering but, if analyzed qualitatively, shows that the approach is promising, even if it must be polished. The second experiment, clustering by author, outperformed the baseline and obtained good enough positive results. Authorship attribution is mostly used for either forensic purposes or plagiarism identification. However, we have shown that an analysis of the features and yielded clustering can also be used to explore structural inter- and intra-similarities among different authors.

8 Acknowledgements

The authors thank the anonymous reviewers for their helpful comments and suggestions.

References

Scott Aaronson. 2001. Stylometric clustering: A comparison of data-driven and syntactic features. Technical report, Computer Science Department, University of California, Berkeley.

Apoorv Agarwal, Augusto Corvalan, Jacob Jensen, and Owen Rambow. 2012. Social network analysis of alice in wonderland. In *Workshop on Computational Linguistics for Literature, Association for Computational Linguistics*, pages 88–96.

Navot Akiva and Moshe Koppel. 2012. Identifying distinct components of a multi-author document. *EISIC*, pages 205–209.

Ricardo Alberich, Josep Miró-Julià, and Francesc Rosselló. 2002. Marvel universe looks almost like a real social network. *cond-mat/*.

Sarah Allison, Ryan Heuser, Matthew Jockers, Franco Moretti, and Michael Witmore. 2011. Quantitative formalism: an experiment. *Literary Lab*, Pamphlet 1.

Harald Baayen, Hans van Halteren, and Fiona Tweedie. 1996. Outside the cave of shadows: using syntactic annotation to enhance authorship attribution. *Literary and Linguistic Computing*, 11:121–131.

Mikhail Bakhtin. 1981. Epic and novel: Towards a methodology for the study of the novel. In J. Michael Holquist, editor, *The dialogic imagination: four essays*. Unversity of Texas Press.

Ron Bekkerman, Hema Raghavan, and James Allan Koji Eguchi. 2007. Interactive clustering of text collections according to a user-specified criterion. In *In Proceedings of IJCAI*, pages 684–689.

Asli Celikyilmaz, Dilek Hakkani-tur, Hua He, Greg Kondrak, and Denilson Barbosa. 2010. The actor-topic model for extracting social networks in literary narrative. In *NIPS Workshop: Machine Learning for Social Computing*.

David K. Elson and Kathleen R. McKeown. 2010. Automatic attribution of quoted speech in literary narrative. In *Association for the Advancement of Artificial Intelligence*.

David K. Elson, Nicholas Dames, and Kathleen R. McKeown. 2010. Extracting social networks from literary fiction. In *Proceedings of the 48th Annual Meeting of the Association for Computational Linguistics*.

Suhit Gupta, Hila Becker, Gail Kaiser, and Salvatore Stolfo. 2005. A genre-based clustering approach to content extraction. Technical report, Department of Computer Science, Columbia University.

Mark Hall, Eibe Frank, Geoffrey Holmes, Bernhard Pfahringer, Peter Reutemann, and Ian H. Witten. 2009. The weka data mining software: An update. *SIGKDD Explorations*, Volume 11.

David I. Holmes and Richard S. Forsyth. 1995. The federalist revisited: New directions in authorship attribution. *Literary and Linguistic Computing*, 10:111–127.

Robert Layton, Paul Watters, and Richard Dazeley. 2011. Automated unsupervised authorship analysis using evidence accumulation clustering. *Natural Language Engineering*, 19:95–120.

Gerard Ledger and Thomas Merriam. 1994. Shakespeare, fletcher, and the two noble kinsmen. *Literary and Linguistic Computing*, 9:235–248.

Franco Moretti. 2011. Network theory, plot analysis. *Literary Lab*, Pamphlet 2.

M. E. J. Newman and M. Girvan. 2003. Finding and evaluating community structure in networks. *Physical Review E*, 69:1–16.

Bohdan Pavlyshenko. 2012. The clustering of author's texts of english fiction in the vector space of semantic fields. *The Computing Research Repository*, abs/1212.1478.

Céline Poudat and Guillaume Cleuziou. 2003. Genre and domain processing in an information retrieval perspective. In *ICWE*, pages 399–402.

Vladimir I. A. Propp. 1968. *Morphology of the folktale*. University of Texas Press.

Jeff Rydberg-Cox. 2011. Social networks and the language of greek tragedy. *Journal of the Chicago Colloquium on Digital Humanities and Computer Science*, 1:1–11.

Graham Alexander Sack. 2011. Simulating plot: Towards a generative model of narrative structure. In *Complex Adaptive Systems: Energy, Information and Intelligence: Papers from the 2011 AAAI Fall Symposium (FS-11-03)*, pages 127–136.

Graham Sack. 2012. Character networks for narrative generation. In *Intelligent Narrative Technologies: Papers from the 2012 AIIDE Workshop, AAAI Technical Report WS-12-14*, pages 38–43.

Caroline Suen, Laney Kuenzel, and Sebastian Gil. 2013. Extraction and analysis of character interaction networks from plays and movies. Retrieved from : http://dh2013.unl.edu/abstracts/ab-251.html, July.

Bin Zhang. 2013. *Learning Features for Text Classification*. Ph.D. thesis, University of Washington.

From Speaker Identification to Affective Analysis: A Multi-Step System for Analyzing Children's Stories

Elias Iosif* **and Taniya Mishra**†
* School of ECE, Technical University of Crete, Chania 73100, Greece
† AT&T Labs, 33 Thomas Street, New York, NY 10007, USA
iosife@telecom.tuc.gr, taniya@research.att.com

Abstract

We propose a multi-step system for the analysis of children's stories that is intended to be part of a larger text-to-speech-based storytelling system. A hybrid approach is adopted, where pattern-based and statistical methods are used along with utilization of external knowledge sources. This system performs the following story analysis tasks: identification of characters in each story; attribution of quotes to specific story characters; identification of character age, gender and other salient personality attributes; and finally, affective analysis of the quoted material. The different types of analyses were evaluated using several datasets. For the quote attribution, as well as for the gender and age estimation, substantial improvement over baseline was realized, whereas results for personality attribute estimation and valence estimation are more modest.

1 Introduction

Children love listening to stories. Listening to stories — read or narrated — has been shown to be positively correlated with children's linguistic and intellectual development (Natsiopoulou et al., 2006). Shared story reading with parents or teachers helps children to learn about vocabulary, syntax and phonology, and to develop narrative comprehension and awareness of the concepts of print, all of which are linked to developing reading and writing skills (National Early Literacy Panel 2008). While acknowledging that the parental role in storytelling is irreplaceable, we consider text-to-speech (TTS) enabled storytelling systems (Rusko et al., 2013; Zhang et al., 2003; Theune et al., 2006) to be aligned with the class of child-oriented applications that aim to aid learning.

For a TTS-based digital storytelling system to successfully create an experience as engaging as human storytelling, the underlying speech synthesis system has to narrate the story in a "storytelling speech style" (Theune et al., 2006), generate dialogs uttered by different characters using synthetic voices appropriate for each character's gender, age and personality (Greene et al., 2012), and express quotes demonstrating emotions such as sadness, fear, happiness, anger and surprise (Alm, 2008) with realistic expression (Murray and Arnott, 2008). However, before any of the aforementioned requirements — all related to speech generation — can be met, the text of the story has to be analyzed to identify which portions of the text should be rendered by the narrator and which by each of the characters in the story, who are the different characters in the story, what is each character's gender, age, or other salient personality attributes that may influence the voice assigned to that character, and what is the expressed affect in each of the character quotes.

Each of these text analysis tasks has been approached in past work (as described in our Related Works section). However, there appears to be no single story analysis system that performs all four of these tasks, which can be pipelined with one of the many currently available text-to-speech systems to build a TTS-based storyteller system. Without such a story analysis system, it will not be possible to develop an engaging and lively digital storyteller system, despite the prevalence of several mature TTS systems.

In this paper, we present a multi-step text analysis system for analyzing children's stories that performs all four analysis tasks: (i) Character Identification, i.e., identifying the different characters in the story, (ii) Quote Attribution, i.e., identifying which portions of the text should be rendered by the narrator versus by particular characters in the story, (iii) Character Attribute Identification, i.e., identifying each character's gender, age, or salient personality attributes that may influence the voice that the speech synthesis system assigns to each character, and (iv) Affective Analysis, i.e., estimating the affect of the character quotes.

This story analysis system was developed to be part of a larger TTS-based storyteller system aimed at children. As a result, the data used for developing the computational models or rules in each step of our system were obtained from children's stories. A majority of children's stories are short. They often contain multiple characters, each with different personalities, genders, age, ethnicities, etc., with some characters even being anthropomorphic, e.g., the singing candlestick or the talking teapot. In addition, there are several prototypical templates characterizing the main characters in the story (Rusko et al., 2013). However, character development is limited in these stories due to the shorter length of text. Overall, children's stories can be regarded as a parsimonious yet fertile framework for developing computational models for literature analysis in general.

2 Related Work

Elson and McKeown (2010) used rule-based and statistical learning approaches to identify candidate characters and attribute each quote to the most likely speaker. Two broad approaches for the identification of story characters were followed: (i) named entity recognition, and (ii) identification of character nominals, e.g., "her grandma", using syntactic patterns. A long list of heuristics for character identification is proposed in (Mamede and Chaleira, 2004). He et al. (2013) use a supervised machine learning approach to address the same problem, though many of their preliminary steps and input features are similar to those used in (Elson and McKeown, 2010). Our character identification and quote attribution is based on syntactic and heuristic rules that is motivated by each of these works.

There are two interesting sub-problems related to quote attribution. First is the problem of identifying anaphoric speakers, i.e., in the utterance *"Hello", he said*, which character is referred to by the pronoun *he*? This problem is addressed in (Elson and McKeown, 2010) and (He et al., 2013) but not in (Mamede and Chaleira, 2004). The second problem is resolving utterance chains with implicit speakers. Elson and McKeown (2010) describe and address two basic types of utterance chains: (i) one-character chains, and (ii) intertwined chains. In these chains of utterances, the speaker is not explicitly mentioned because the author relies on the shared understanding with the reader that adjacent pieces of quoted speech are not independent (Zhang et al., 2003; Elson and McKeown, 2010). They are either a continuation of the same character's speech (one-character chains) or a dialogue between the two characters (intertwined chains). In (Zhang et al., 2003), the quote-identification module detects whether a piece of quoted speech is a new quote (NEW), spoken by a speaker different from the previous speaker, or a continuation quote (CONT) spoken by the same speaker as that of the previous quote. He et al. (2013) also identified similar chains of utterances and addressed their attribution to characters using a model-based approach. In this work, we address both sub-problems, namely, anaphoric speaker and implicit speaker identification.

Cabral et al. (2006) have shown that assigning an appropriate voice for a character in a digital storyteller system is significant for understanding a story, perceiving affective content, perceiving the voice as credible, and overall listener satisfaction. Greene et al. (2012) have shown that the appropriateness of the voice assigned to a synthetic character is strongly related to knowing the gender, age and other salient personality attributes of the character. Given this, we have developed rule-based, machine-learning-based and resource-based approaches for estimation of character gender, age and salient personality attributes. In contrast, the majority of past works on the analysis of children stories for TTS-based storytelling is limited to the attribution of quotes to speakers, though studies that focused on anaphoric speaker identification have also approached character gender estimation such as (Elson and McKeown, 2010) and (He et al., 2013). The utilization of available resources containing associations between person names and gender was followed in (Elson and

McKeown, 2010). In (He et al., 2013), associations between characters and their gender were performed using anaphora rules (Mitkov, 2002).

There is of course a significant body of work from other research areas that are related to the estimation of character attributes, similar to what we have attempted in our work. Several shallow linguistic features were proposed in (Schler et al., 2006) for gender identification, applied to the identification of users in social media. Several socio-linguistic features were proposed in (Rao et al., 2010) for estimating the age and gender of Twitter users. The identification of personality attributes from text is often motivated by psychological models. In (Celli, 2012), a list of linguistic features were used for the creation of character models in terms of the the Big Five personality dimensions (Norman, 1963).

Analysis of text to estimate affect or sentiment is a relatively recent research topic that has attracted great interest, as reflected by a series of shared evaluation tasks, e.g., analysis of news headlines (Strapparava and Mihalcea, 2007) and tweets (Nakov et al., 2013). Relevant applications deal with numerous domains such as blogs (Balog et al., 2006), news stories (Lloyd et al., 2005), and product reviews (Hu and Liu, 2004). In (Turney and Littman, 2002), the affective ratings of unknown words were predicted using the affective ratings for a small set of words (seeds) and the semantic relatedness between the unknown and the seed words. An example of sentence-level analysis was proposed in (Malandrakis et al., 2013). In (Alm et al., 2005) and (Alm, 2008), linguistic features were used for affect analysis in fairy tales. In our work, we employ a feature set similar to that in (Alm et al., 2005). We deal with the prediction of three basic affective labels which are adequate for the intended application (i.e., storytelling system), while in (Alm, 2008) more fine-grained predictions are considered.

The integration of various types of analysis constitutes the distinguishing character of our work.

3 Overview of System Architecture

The system consists of several sub-systems that are linked in a pipeline. The input to the system is simply the text of a story with no additional annotation. The story analysis is performed sequentially, with each sub-system extracting specific information needed to perform the four analysis tasks laid out in this paper.

3.1 Linguistic Preprocessing

The first step is linguistic pre-processing of the stories. This includes (i) tokenization, (ii) sentence splitting and identification of paragraph boundaries, (iii) part-of-speech (POS) tagging, (iv) lemmatization, (v) named entity recognition, (vi) dependency parsing, and (vii) co-reference analysis. These sub-tasks — except task (ii) — were performed using the Stanford CoreNLP suite of tools (CoreNLP, 2014). Sentence splitting and identification of paragraph boundaries was performed using a splitter developed by Piao (2014). Linguistic information extracted by this analysis is exploited by the subsequent parts of the pipeline.

3.2 Identification of Story Characters

The second step is identifying candidate characters (i.e., entities) that appear in the stories under analysis. A story character is not necessarily a story speaker. A character may appear in the story but may not have any quote associated with him and hence, is not a speaker. Characters in children's stories can either be human or non-human entities, i.e., animals and non-living objects, exhibiting anthropomorphic traits. The interactions among characters can either be human-to-human or human-to-non-human interactions.

We used two approaches for identifying story characters motivated by (Elson and McKeown, 2010): 1) named entity recognition was used for identifying proper names, e.g., "Hansel", 2) a set of part-of-speech patterns was used for the extraction of human and non-human characters that were not represented by proper names, e.g., "wolf". The used patterns are: 1) `(DT|CD) (NN|NNS)`, 2) `DT JJ (NN|NNS)`, 3) `NN POS (NN|NNS)`, and 4) `PRP$ JJ (NN|NNS)`.

These POS-based patterns are quite generic, allowing for the creation of large sets of characters. In order to restrict the characters, world knowledge was incorporated through the use of WordNet (Fellbaum, 2005). A similar approach was also followed in (Elson and McKeown, 2010). For each candidate character the hierarchy of its hypernyms was traversed up to the root. Regarding polysemous characters the first two senses were considered. A character was retained if any of its hypernyms was found to fall into certain types of WordNet concepts: person, animal, plant, artifact, spiritual being, physical entity.

3.3 Quote Attribution & Speaker Identification

Here the goal is to attribute (or assign) each quote to a specific story character from the set identified in the previous step. The identification of quotes in the story is based on a simple pattern-based approach: the quote boundaries are signified by the respective symbols, e.g., “ and ”. The pattern is applied at the sentence level.

The quotes are not modeled as NEW/CONT as in (Zhang et al., 2003), however, we adopt a more sophisticated approach for the quote attribution. Three types of attribution are possible in our system: 1) explicit mention of speakers, e.g., “Done!” **said** Hans, merrily, 2) anaphoric mention of speakers, e.g., “How happy am I!” **cried** he, 3) sequence of quotes, e.g., “And where did you get the pig?” ... “I gave a horse for it.”. In the first type of attribution, the speaker is explicitly mentioned in the *vicinity* of the quote. This is also true for the second type, however, a pronominal anaphora is used to refer to the the speaker. The first two attribution types are characterized by the presence of “within-quote” (e.g., “Done!”) and “out-of-quote” (e.g., “said Hans, merrily.”) content. This is not the case for the third attribution type for which only “in-quote” content is available. We refer to such quotes as “pure” quotes. Each attribution type is detailed below.

Preliminary filtering of characters. Before quote-attribution is performed, the list of story characters is pruned by identifying the characters that are “passively” associated with *speech verbs* (SV). This is applied at the sentence level. Some examples of speech verbs are: said, responds, sing, etc. For instance, in “... Hans was **told** ...”, “Hans” is a passive character. The passive characters were identified via the following relations extracted by dependency parsing: `nsubjpass` (passive nominal subject) and `pobj` (object of a preposition). Given a sentence that includes one or more quotes, the respective passive characters were not considered as candidate speakers. Some other criteria for pruning of list of characters to identify candidate speakers are presented in Section 4.2 (see the three schemes for Tasks 1-2).

Explicit mention of speakers. Several syntactic patterns were applied to associate quotes with explicit mention of speakers in their vicinity to characters from the pruned list of story characters. These patterns were developed around SV. In the example above, “Hans” is associated with the quote “Done!” via the SV “said”. Variations of the following basic patterns (Elson and McKeown, 2010) were used: 1) `QT SV CH`, 2) `QT CH SV`, and 3) `CH SV QT`, where QT denotes a quote boundary and CH stands for a story character. For example, a variation of the first pattern is `QT SV the? CH`, where `?` stands for zero or one occurrence of “the”.

A limitation of the aforementioned patterns is that they capture associations when the CH and SV occur in close textual distance. As a result, distant associations are missed, e.g., “Hans stood looking on for a while, and at last **said**, “ You must ...””. In order to address this distant association issue, we examined the `collapsed-ccprocessed-dependencies` output besides the `basic-dependencies` output of the Stanford CoreNLP dependency engine (de Marneffe and Manning, 2012). The former captures more distant relations compared to the latter. We specifically extract the character reference CH either from the dependency relation *nsubj*, which links a speech verb SV with a CH that is the syntactic subject of a clause, or from the dependency relation *dobj*, which links a SV with a CH that is the direct object of the speech verb, across a conjunct (e.g., and). A similar approach was used in (He et al., 2013).

Anaphoric mention of speakers. The same procedure was followed as in the case of the explicit mentions of speakers described above. The difference is that CH included the following pronouns: “he”, “she”, “they”, “himself”, “herself”, and “themselves”. After associating a pronoun with a quote, the quote was attributed to a story character via co-reference resolution. This was done using the co-reference analysis performed by CoreNLP. If a pronominal anaphora was not resolved by the CoreNLP analysis, the following heuristic was adopted. The previous n paragraphs[1] were searched and the pronoun under investigation was mapped to the closest (in terms of textual proximity) story character that had the same gender as the pronoun (see Section 3.4.1 regarding gender estimation). During the paragraph search, anaphoric mentions were also taken into consideration followed by co-reference resolution.

Despite the above approaches, it is possible to have non-attributed quotes. In such cases, the fol-

[1]For the reported results n was set to 5.

lowing procedure is followed for those story sentences that: (i) do not constitute "pure" quotes (i.e., consist of "in-quote" and "out-of-quote" content), and (ii) include at least one "out-of-quote" SV: 1) all the characters (as well as pronouns) that occur within the "out-of-quote" content are aggregated and serve as valid candidates for attribution, 2) if multiple characters and pronouns exist, then they are mapped (if possible) via co-reference resolution in order to narrow down the list of attribution candidates, and 3) the quote is attributed to the nearest quote character (or pronoun). For the computation of the textual distance both quote boundaries (i.e., start and end) are considered. If the quote is attributed to a pronoun that was not mapped to any character, then co-reference resolution is applied.

Sequence of "pure" quotes. Sentences that are "pure" quotes (i.e., include "in-quote" content only) are not attributed to any story character via the last two attribution methods. "Pure" quotes are attributed as follows: The sentences are parsed sequentially starting from the beginning of the story. Each time a character is encountered within a sentence, it is pushed into a "bag-of-characters". This is done until a non-attributed "pure" quote is found. At this point we assume that the candidate speakers for the current (and next) "pure" quote are included within the "bag-of-characters". This is based on the hypothesis that the author "introduces" the speakers before their utterances. The subsequent "pure" quotes are examined in order to spot any included characters. Such characters are regarded as "good" candidates enabling the pruning of the list of candidate speakers. The goal is to end up with exactly two candidate speakers for a back and forth dialogue. Then, the initiating speaker is identified by taking into account the order of names mentioned within the quote. Then, the quote attribution is performed in an alternating fashion. For example, consider a sequence of four non-attributed "pure" quotes and a bag of two[2] candidate speakers, s_i and s_j. If s_i was identified as the initiating speaker, then the 1st and the 3th quote are attributed to it, while the 2nd and the 4th quote are attributed to s_j. Finally, the "bag-of-characters" is reset, and the same process is repeated for the rest of the story.

Identification of speakers. The speakers for a given story are identified by selecting those characters that were attributed at least one quote.

3.4 Gender, Age and Personality Attributes

The next three steps in our system involve estimation of the (i) gender, (ii) age, and (iii) personality attributes for the identified speakers.

3.4.1 Gender Estimation

We used a hybrid approach for estimating the gender of the story characters. This is applied to characters (rather than only speakers) because the gender information is exploited during the attribution of quotes (see Section 3.3). The characterization "hybrid" refers to the fusion of two different types of information: (i) linguistic information extracted from the story under analysis, and (ii) information taken from external resources that do not depend on the analyzed story. Regarding the story-specific information, the associations between characters and third person pronouns (identified via anaphora resolution) were counted. The counts were used in order to estimate the gender probability.

The story-independent resources that we used are: (a) the U.S. Social Security Administration baby name database (Security, 2014), in which person names are linked with gender and (b) a large name-gender association list developed using a corpus-based bootstrapping approach, which even included the estimated gender for non-person entities (Bergsma and Lin, 2006). For each entity included in (b) a numerical estimate is provided for each gender. As in the case of story-specific information, those estimates were utilized for computing the gender probability. Using the above information the following procedure was followed for each character: The external resource (a) was used when the character name occurred in it. Otherwise, the information from the external resource (b) and the story-specific information was taken into account. If the speaker was covered by both types of information, the respective gender probabilities were compared and the gender was estimated to be the one corresponding to the highest probability. If the character was not covered by the story-specific information, the external resource (b) was used.

3.4.2 Age Estimation

We used a machine-learning based approach for age estimation. The used features are presented in Table 1, while they were extracted from speaker

[2] If more than two candidates exist, then the system gives ambiguous attributions, i.e., multiple speakers for one quote.

quotes, based on the assumption that speakers of different ages use language differently. The development of this feature set was inspired by (Celli, 2012) and (Alm et al., 2005). All features were extracted from the lemmatized form of quotes. Also, all feature counts (except Feature 21) were normalized by Feature 12. For computing the counts of positive and negative words (Feature 15 and 16) we used the General Inquirer database (Stone et al., 1966). Feature 21 stands for n-grams (up to 3-grams) extracted from the speaker quotes. Two different schemes were followed for extracting this feature: (i) using the quote as-is, i.e., its lexical form, and (ii) using the part-of-speech tags of quote. So, two slightly different feature sets were defined: 1) "lex": No.1-20 + lexical form for No.21, 2) "pos": No.1-20 + POS tags for No.21

No.	Description
1	count of . , ;
2	count of ,
3	count of !
4	count of 1st person singular pronouns
5	count of negative particles
6	count of numbers
7	count of prepositions
8	count of pronouns
9	count of ?
10	count of tokens longer than 6 letters
11	count of 1st pers. (sing. & plur.) pronouns
12	count of quote tokens
13	count of 1st person plural pronouns
14	count of 2nd person singular pronouns
15	count of quote positive words
16	count of quote negative words
17	count of nouns
18	count of verbs
19	count of adjectives
20	count of adverbs
21	up to 3-grams extracted from quote

Table 1: Common feature set.

3.4.3 Estimation of Personality Attributes

A machine-learning based approach was also used for personality attribute estimation. For estimating the personality attributes of story speakers, the linguistic feature set (see Table 1) used in the task for age estimation was used again . Again our approach was based on the assumption that words people use reflect their personality, and the latter can be estimated by these linguistic features.

3.5 Affective Analysis

The last step of our system is the estimation of the affective content of stories. The analysis is performed for each identified quote. The features presented in Table 1 are extracted for each quote and affect is estimated using a machine-learning model, based on the assumption that such features serve as cues for revealing the underlying affective content (Alm et al., 2005; Alm, 2008).

4 Experiments and Evaluation

Here we present the experimental evaluation of our system in performing the following tasks: 1) speaker-to-quote attribution, 2) gender estimation, 3) age estimation, 4) identification of personality attributes, and 5) affective analysis of stories.

4.1 Datasets Used

The datasets used for our experiments along with the related tasks are presented in Table 2.

No.	Task	Type of dataset
1	Quote attribution	STORIES
2	Gender estimation	STORIES
3	Age estimation	QUOTES(1,2)
4	Personality attrib.	QUOTES(3,4)
5	Affective analysis	STORY-AFFECT

Table 2: Experiment datasets and related tasks.

Tasks 1-2. For the first two tasks (quote-to-speaker attribution, and gender estimation) we used a dataset (STORIES) consisting of 17 children stories selected from Project Gutenberg[3]. This set of stories includes 98 unique speakers with 554 quotes assigned to them. The average number of sentences and quotes per story is 61.8 and 32.5, respectively. The average sentence and quote length is 30.4 and 29.0 tokens, respectively. Each speaker was attributed 5.7 quotes on average. Ground truth annotation, which involved assigning quotes to speakers and labeling gender, was performed by one[4] annotator. The following ground truth labels were used to mark gender: "male", "female", and "plural".

[3] www.telecom.tuc.gr/~iosife/chst.html

[4] Due to the limited ambiguity of the task, the availability of a single annotator was considered acceptable.

Task 3. Evaluation of the age estimation task was performed with respect to two different (proprietary) datasets QUOTES1 and QUOTES2. These datasets consisted of individual quotes assigned to popular children's story characters. The dataset QUOTES1 consisted of 6361 quotes assigned to 69 unique speakers. The average quote length equals 7.6 tokens, while each speaker was attributed 141.4 quotes on average. The dataset QUOTES2 consisted of 23605 quotes assigned to 262 unique speakers. The average quote length equals 8.3 tokens, while each speaker was attributed 142.6 quotes on average. For ground truth annotation, four annotators were employed. The annotators were asked to use the following age labels: "child" (0–15 years old), "young adult" (16–35 y.o.), "middle-aged" (36–55 y.o.), and "elderly" (56– y.o.). The age of each character was inferred by the annotators either based on personal knowledge of these stories or by consulting publicly available sources online. The inter-annotator agreement equals to 70%.

Task 4. To evaluate system performance on Task 4, two datasets QUOTES3 and QUOTES4, consisting of individual quotes assigned to popular children's story characters, were used. The set QUOTES3 consisted of 68 individual characters and QUOTES4 consisted of 328 individual characters. The ground truth assignment, assigning each character with personality attributes, was extracted from a free, public collaborative wiki (Wiki, 2014). Since the wiki format allows people to add or edit information, we considered the personality attributes extracted from this wiki to be the average "crowd's opinion" of these characters. Of the open-ended list of attributes that were used to describe the characters, in this task we attempted to extract the following salient personality attributes: "beautiful", "brave", "cowardly", "evil", "feisty", "greedy", "handsome", "kind", "loving", "loyal", "motherly", "optimistic", "spunky", "sweet", and "wise". The pseudo-attribute "none" was used when a character was not described with any of those aforementioned attributes.

Task 5. An annotated dataset, referred to as STORY-AFFECT in this paper, consisting of 176 stories was used. Each story sentence (regardless if quotes were included or not) was annotated regarding primary emotions and mood using the following labels: "angry" (AN), "disgusted" (DI), "fearful" (FE), "happy" (HA), "neutral" (NE), "sad" (SA), "positive surprise" (SU^{+}), and "negative surprise" (SU^{-}). Overall, two annotators were employed, while each annotator provided two annotations: one for emotion and one for mood. More details about this dataset are provided in (Alm, 2008).

Instead of using the aforementioned emotions/moods as annotated, we adopted a 3-class scheme for sentence affect (valence): "negative", "neutral", and "positive". In order to align the existing annotations to our three-class scheme the following mapping[5] was adopted: (i) AN, DI, FE, SA were mapped to negative affect, (ii) NE was mapped to neutral affect, and (iii) HA was mapped to positive affect. Given the proposed mapping, we retained those sentences (in total 11018) that exhibited at least 75% annotation agreement.

4.2 Evaluation Results

The evaluation results for the aforementioned tasks are presented below.

Tasks 1-2. The quote-to-speaker attribution was evaluated in terms of precision (AT_p), while the estimation of speakers' gender was evaluated in terms of precision (G_p) and recall (G_r). Note that G_p includes both types of errors: (i) erroneous age estimation, and (ii) estimations for story characters that are not true speakers. In order to exclude the second type of error, the precision of gender estimation was also computed for only the true story speaker identified by the system ($G_p^{'}$). For

Speaker filter.	AT_p	G_p	G_r	$G_p^{'}$
Baseline	0.010	0.333		
10 stories (subset of dataset)				
Scheme 1	0.833	0.780	0.672	0.929
Scheme 2	0.868	0.710	0.759	0.917
Scheme 3	0.835	0.710	0.759	0.917
17 stories (full dataset)				
Scheme 2	0.845	0.688	0.733	0.892

Table 3: Quote attribution and gender estimation.

a subset of the STORIES dataset that included 10 stories, the following schemes were used for filtering of candidate speakers: (i) Scheme 1: all speakers linked with speech verbs, (ii) Scheme 2: speakers, who are persons or animals or spiritual entities according to their first WordNet sense, linked with speech verbs , and (iii) Scheme 3: as Scheme 2,

[5] $SU^{+/-}$ were excluded for simplicity.

but the first two WordNet senses were considered. For the full STORIES dataset (17 stories) Scheme 2 was used. The results are presented in Table 3 including the weighted averages of precision and recall. Using random guesses, the baseline precision is 0.010 and 0.333 for quote-to-speaker attribution and gender estimation, respectively. For the subset of 10 stories, the highest speaker-to-quote attribution attribution is obtained by Scheme 2. When this scheme is applied over the entire dataset, substantially high[6] precision (0.892) is achieved in the estimation of gender of true story speakers.

Task 3. For the estimation of age using quote-based features, a boosting approach was followed using BoosTexter (Schapire and Singer, 2000). For evaluation, 10-fold cross validation (10FCV) was used for the QUOTES1 and QUOTES2 datasets for the "lex" and "pos" feature sets. The results are reported in Table 4 in terms of average classification accuracy. In this table, BOTH refers to the datasets QUOTES1 and QUOTES2 combined together. The evaluation was performed according to two schemes: (i) "relaxed match": the prediction is considered as correct even if it deviates one class from the true one, e.g., "child" and "middle-aged" considered as correct for "young adult", and (ii) "exact match": the prediction should exactly match the true label. The relaxed scheme was motivated by the nature of intended application (storytelling system) for which such errors are tolerable. For the exact match scheme, the obtained performance is higher[7] than the baseline (random guess) that equals to 0.250. The accuracy for the relaxed scheme is quite high, i.e., greater than 0.85 for almost all cases. On average, the "lex" feature set appears to yield slightly higher performance than the "pos" set.

Dataset	Relaxed		Exact	
	lex	pos	lex	pos
Baseline	0.625		0.250	
QUOTES1	0.869	0.883	0.445	0.373
QUOTES2	0.877	0.831	0.450	0.435
BOTH	0.886	0.858	0.464	0.383

Table 4: Age estimation: average accuracy.

Task 4. The personality attributes were estimated using BoosTexter fed with the "lex" feature set. 10FCV was used for evaluation, while the average accuracy was computed by taking into account the top five attributes predicted for each character. The baseline accuracy equals 0.31 given that random guesses are used. Moderate performance was achieved for the QUOTES3 and QUOTES4 datasets, 0.426 and 0.411, respectively.

Task 5. The affect of story sentences was estimated via BoosTexter using the "lex" and "pos" feature sets. As in the previous two tasks 10FCV was applied for evaluation purposes. Using random guesses, the baseline accuracy is 0.33. The average accuracy for the "lex" and "pos" feature sets is 0.838 and 0.658, respectively[8]. It is clear that the use of the "lex" set outperforms the results yielded by the "pos" set.

5 Conclusions and Future Directions

In this paper, we described the development of a multi-step system aimed for story analysis with particular emphasis on analyzing children's stories. The core idea was the integration of several systems into a single pipelined system. The proposed methodology has a strong hybrid character in that it employs different approaches that range from pattern-based to machine learning-based to the incorporation of external knowledge resources. Going beyond the usual task of works in this genre, i.e., speaker-to-quote attribution, the proposed system also supports the estimation of speaker-oriented attributes and affect estimation. Very promising results were obtained for quote attribution and estimation of speaker gender, as well as for age assuming an application-depended error tolerance. The estimation of personality attributes and the affective analysis of story sentences remain open research problems, while the results are more modest especially for the former task.

In the next phase of our work, we hope to improve and generalize each individual component of the proposed system. The most challenging aspects of the system, dealing with personality attributes and affective analysis, will be further investigated. Towards this task, psychological models, e.g., the Big Five model, can provide useful theoretical and empirical findings. Last but not least, the proposed system will be evaluated within the framework of a digital storytelling application including metrics related with user experience.

[6]Statistically significant at 95% lev. (t-test wrt baseline).

[7]Statistically significant at 95% lev. (t-test wrt baseline).

[8]Statistically significant at 90% lev. (t-test wrt baseline).

References

C. O. Alm, D. Roth, and R. Sproat. 2005. Emotions from text: Machine learning for text-based emotion prediction. In *Proc. of Conference on Human Language Technology and Empirical Methods in Natural Language Processing*, pages 579–586.

C. O. Alm. 2008. *Affect in Text and Speech*. Ph.D. thesis, University of Illinois at Urbana-Champaign.

K. Balog, G. Mishne, and M. de Rijke. 2006. Why are they excited? identifying and explaining spikes in blog mood levels. In *Proc. 11th Conference of the European Chapter of the Association for Computational Linguistics*, pages 207–210.

S. Bergsma and D. Lin. 2006. Bootstrapping path-based pronoun resolution. In *Proc. of Conference on Computational Lingustics / Association for Computational Linguistics*, pages 33–40.

J. Cabral, L. Oliveira, G. Raimundo, and A. Paiva. 2006. What voice do we expect from a synthetic character? In *Proceedings of SPECOM*, pages 536–539.

F. Celli. 2012. Unsupervised personality recognition for social network sites. In *Proc. of Sixth International Conference on Digital Society*.

CoreNLP. 2014. Stanford CoreNLP tool. `http://nlp.stanford.edu/software/corenlp.shtml`.

M.-C. de Marneffe and C. D. Manning. 2012. Stanford typed dependencies manual.

D. K. Elson and K. R. McKeown. 2010. Automatic attribution of quoted speech in literary narrative. In *Proc. of Twenty-Fourth AAAI Conference on Artificial Intelligence*.

C. Fellbaum. 2005. Wordnet and wordnets. In K. Brown et al., editor, *Encyclopedia of Language and Linguistics*, pages 665–670. Oxford: Elsevier.

E. Greene, T. Mishra, P. Haffner, and A. Conkie. 2012. Predicting character-appropriate voices for a TTS-based storyteller system. In *Proc. of Interspeech*.

H. He, D. Barbosa, and G. Kondrak. 2013. Identification of speakers in novels. In *Proc. of 51st Annual Meeting of the Association for Computational Linguistics*, pages 1312–1320.

M. Hu and B. Liu. 2004. Mining and summarizing customer reviews. In *Proc. of Conference on Knowledge Discovery and Data Mining*, KDD '04, pages 168–177.

L. Lloyd, D. Kechagias, and S. Skiena. 2005. Lydia: A system for large-scale news analysis. In *Proc. SPIRE*, number 3772 in Lecture Notes in Computer Science, pages 161–166.

N. Malandrakis, A. Potamianos, E. Iosif, and S. Narayanan. 2013. Distributional semantic models for affective text analysis. *IEEE Transactions on Audio, Speech, and Language Processing*, 21(11):2379–2392.

N. Mamede and P. Chaleira. 2004. Character identification in children stories. In J. Vicedo, P. Martnez-Barco, R. Muoz, and M. Saiz Noeda, editors, *Advances in Natural Language Processing*, volume 3230 of *Lecture Notes in Computer Science*, pages 82–90. Springer Berlin Heidelberg.

R. Mitkov. 2002. *Anaphora Resolution*. Longman.

I. R. Murray and J. L. Arnott. 2008. Applying an analysis of acted vocal emotions to improve the simulation of synthetic speech. *Computer Speech and Language*, 22(2):107–129.

P. Nakov, S. Rosenthal, Z. Kozareva, V. Stoyanov, A. Ritter, and T. Wilson. 2013. Semeval 2013 task 2: Sentiment analysis in twitter. In *Proc. of Second Joint Conference on Lexical and Computational Semantics (*SEM), Seventh International Workshop on Semantic Evaluation*, pages 312–320.

T. Natsiopoulou, M. Souliotis, and A. G. Kyridis. 2006. Narrating and reading folktales and picture books: storytelling techniques and approaches with preschool children. *Early Childhood Research and Practice*, 8(1). Retrieved on Jan 13th, 2014 from `http://ecrp.uiuc.edu/v8n1/natsiopoulou.html`.

T. W. Norman. 1963. Toward an adequate taxonomy of personality attributes: Replicated factor structure in peer nomination personality rating. *Journal of Abnormal and Social Psychology*, 66:574–583.

S. Piao. 2014. Sentence splitting program. `http://text0.mib.man.ac.uk:8080/scottpiao/sent_detector`.

D. Rao, D. Yarowsky, A. Shreevats, and M. Gupta. 2010. Classifying latent user attributes in twitter. In *Proc. of the 2nd International Workshop on Search and Mining User-generated Contents*, pages 37–44.

M. Rusko, M. Trnka, S. Darjaa, and J. Hamar. 2013. The dramatic piece reader for the blind and visually impaired. In *Proc. of 4th Workshop on Speech and Language Processing for Assistive Technologies*, pages 83–91.

R. E. Schapire and Y. Singer. 2000. Boostexter: A boosting-based system for text categorization. *Machine. Learning*, 39(2-3):135–168.

J. Schler, M. Koppel, S. Argamon, and J. W. Pennebaker. 2006. Effects of age and gender on blogging. In *Proc. of AAAI Spring Symposium: Computational Approaches to Analyzing Weblogs*.

Social Security. 2014. U.S. social security administration baby name database. `http://www.ssa.gov/OACT/babynames/limits.html`.

P. J. Stone, D. C. Dunphy, M. S. Smith, and D. M. Ogilvie. 1966. *The General Inquirer: A Computer Approach to Content Analysis*. MIT Press.

C. Strapparava and R. Mihalcea. 2007. Semeval 2007 task 14: Affective text. In *Proc. SemEval*, pages 70–74.

M. Theune, K. Meijs, and D. Heylen. 2006. Generating expressive speech for storytelling applications. In *IEEE Transactions on Audio, Speech and Language Processing*, pages 1137–1144.

P. Turney and M. L. Littman. 2002. Unsupervised learning of semantic orientation from a hundred-billion-word corpus (technical report erc-1094).

Disney Wiki. 2014. Description of Disney characters. `http://disney.wikia.com/wiki/Category:Disney_characters#`.

J. Y. Zhang, A. W. Black, and R. Sproat. 2003. Identifying speakers in children's stories for speech synthesis. In *Proc. of Interspeech*.

Parsing Screenplays for Extracting Social Networks from Movies

Apoorv Agarwal[†], **Sriramkumar Balasubramanian**[†], **Jiehan Zheng**[‡], **Sarthak Dash**[†]

[†]**Dept. of Computer Science**
Columbia University
New York, NY, USA

[‡]**Peddie School**
Hightstown, NJ, USA

apoorv@cs.columbia.edu

jzheng-14@peddie.org

Abstract

In this paper, we present a formalization of the task of parsing movie screenplays. While researchers have previously motivated the need for parsing movie screenplays, to the best of our knowledge, there is no work that has presented an evaluation for the task. Moreover, all the approaches in the literature thus far have been regular expression based. In this paper, we present an NLP and ML based approach to the task, and show that this approach outperforms the regular expression based approach by a large and statistically significant margin. One of the main challenges we faced early on was the absence of training and test data. We propose a methodology for using well structured screenplays to create training data for anticipated *anomalies* in the structure of screenplays.

1 Introduction

Social network extraction from unstructured text has recently gained much attention (Agarwal and Rambow, 2010; Elson et al., 2010; Agarwal et al., 2013a; Agarwal et al., 2013b; He et al., 2013). Using Natural Language Processing (NLP) and Machine Learning (ML) techniques, researchers are now able to gain access to networks that are not associated with any meta-data (such as email links and self-declared friendship links). Movies, which can be seen as visual approximations of unstructured literary works, contain rich social networks formed by interactions between characters. There has been some effort in the past to extract social networks from movies (Weng et al., 2006; Weng et al., 2007; Weng et al., 2009; Gil et al., 2011). However, these approaches are primarily regular expression based with no evaluation of how well they work.

In this paper we introduce a formalization of the task of parsing screenplays and present an NLP and ML based approach to the task. By parsing a screenplay, we mean assigning each line of the screenplay one of the following five tags: "S" for scene boundary, "N" for scene description, "C" for character name, "D" for dialogue, and "M" for meta-data. We expect screenplays to conform to a strict grammar but they often do not (Gil et al., 2011). This disconnect gives rise to the need for developing a methodology that is able to handle anomalies in the structure of screenplays. Though the methodology proposed in this paper is in the context of movie screenplays, we believe, it is general and applicable to parse other kinds of noisy documents.

One of the earliest challenges we faced was the absence of training and test data. Screenplays, on average, have 7,000 lines of text, which limits the amount of annotated data we can obtain from humans. We propose a methodology for using well structured screenplays to create training data for anticipated *anomalies* in the structure of screenplays. For different types of anomalies, we train separate classifiers, and combine them using ensemble learning. We show that our ensemble outperforms a regular-expression baseline by a large and statistically significant margin on an unseen test set (0.69 versus 0.96 macro-F1 measure for the five classes). Apart from performing an intrinsic evaluation, we also present an extrinsic evaluation. We show that the social network extracted from the screenplay tagged by our ensemble is *closer* to the network extracted from a screenplay tagged by a human, as compared to the network extracted from a screenplay tagged by the baseline.

The rest of the paper is structured as follows: in section 2, we present common terminology used to describe screenplays. We survey existing literature in section 3. Section 4 presents details of our data collection methodology, along with the data distribution. Section 5 gives details of our regular-expression based system, which we use as a baseline for evaluation purposes. In section 6, we present our machine learning approach. In section 7, we give details of the features we use for machine learning. In section 8, we present our experiments and results. We conclude and give future directions of research in section 9.

2 Terminology

Turetsky and Dimitrova (2004) describe the structure of a movie screenplay as follows: a screenplay describes a story, characters, action, setting and dialogue of a film. Additionally, they report that the structure of a screenplay follows a (semi) regular format. Figure 1 shows a snippet of a screenplay from the film – *The Silence of the Lambs*. A scene (tag "S") starts with what is called the *slug line* (or scene boundary). The slug line indicates whether the scene is to take place inside or outside (INT, EXT), the name of the location ("FBI ACADEMY GROUNDS, QUANTICO, VIRGINIA"), and can potentially specify the time of day (e.g. DAY or NIGHT). Following the scene boundary is a scene description. A scene description is followed by a character name (tag "C"), which is followed by dialogues (tag "D"). Character names are capitalized, with an optional (V.O.) for "Voice Over" or (O.S.) for "Off-screen." Dialogues, like scene descriptions, are not associated with any explicit indicators (such as INT, V.O.), but are indented at a unique level (i.e. nothing else in the screenplay is indented at this level). Screenplays may also have other elements, such as "CUT TO:", which are directions for the camera, and text describing the intended mood of the speaker, which is found within parentheses in the dialogue. For lack of a name for these elements, we call them "Meta-data" (tag "M").

3 Literature Survey

One of the earliest works motivating the need for screenplay parsing is that of Turetsky and Dimitrova (2004). Turetsky and Dimitrova (2004) proposed a system to automatically align written screenplays with their videos. One of the crucial steps, they noted, is to parse a screenplay into its different elements: scene boundaries, scene descriptions, character names, and dialogues. They proposed a grammar to parse screenplays and show results for aligning *one* screenplay with its video. Weng et al. (2009) motivated the need for screenplay parsing from a social network analysis perspective. They proposed a set of operations on social networks extracted from movies and television shows in order to find what they called *hidden semantic* information. They proposed techniques for identifying lead roles in *bilateral* movies (movies with two main characters), for performing community analysis, and for automating the task of story segmentation. Gil et al. (2011) extracted character interaction networks from plays and movies. They were interested in automatically classifying plays and movies into different genres by making use of social network analysis metrics. They acknowledged that the scripts found on the internet are not in consistent formats, and proposed a regular expression based system to identify scene boundaries and character names.

While there is motivation in the literature to parse screenplays, none of the aforementioned work addresses the task formally. In this paper, we formalize the task and propose a machine learning based approach that is significantly more effective and tolerant of anomalous structure than the baseline. We evaluate our models on their ability to identify scene boundaries and character names, but also on their ability to identify other important elements of a screenplay, such as scene descriptions and dialogues.

4 Data

We crawled the Internet Movie Script Database (IMSDB) website[1] to collect movie screenplays. We crawled a total of 674 movies. Movies that are well structured have the property that scene boundaries and scene descriptions, character names, and dialogues are all at different but fixed levels of indentation.[2] For example, in the movie in Figure 1, all scene boundaries and scene

[1]http://www.imsdb.com

[2]By level of indentation we mean the number of spaces from the start of the line to the first non-space character.

```
M|                CUT TO:
 |
S|   EXT. FBI ACADEMY GROUNDS, QUANTICO, VIRGINIA - DAY
 |
N|   Crawford is watching a group of trainees on the firing range,
N|   as Clarice joins him. He looks tired, haunted. Between master <---\
N|   and student.                                                       |
 |                                                   [context = -2] |
C|                  CRAWFORD ====================================|
D|      Starling, Clarice M., good morning.                             |
 |                                                   [context = +3] |
C|                  CLARICE                                             |
D|      Good morning, Mr. Crawford. <----------------------------------/
 |
C|                  CRAWFORD
M|                  (sternly)
D|      Your instructors tell me you're doing
D|      well. Top quarter of the class.
```

Figure 1: Example screenplay: first column shows the tags we assign to each line in the screenplay. M stands for "Meta-data", S stands for "Scene boundary", N stands for "Scene description", C stands for "Character name", and D stands for "Dialogue." We also show the lines that are at context -2 and +3 for the line "CRAWFORD."

descriptions are at the same level of indentation, equal to five spaces. All character names are at a different but fixed level of indentation, equal to 20 spaces. Dialogues are at an indentation level of eight spaces. These indentation levels may vary from one screenplay to the other, but are consistent within a well formatted screenplay. Moreover, the indentation level of character names is strictly greater than the indentation level of dialogues, which is strictly greater than the indentation level of scene boundaries and scene descriptions. For each crawled screenplay, we found the frequency of unique indentation levels in that screenplay. If the top three unique frequencies constituted 90% of the total lines of a screenplay, we flagged that the movie was well-structured, and assigned tags based on indentation levels. Since scene boundaries and scene descriptions are at the same level of indentation, we disambiguate between them by utilizing the fact that scene boundaries in well-formatted screenplays start with tags such as INT. and EXT. We programmatically checked the *sanity* of these automatically tagged screenplays by using the following procedure: 1) check if scene descriptions are between scene boundaries and character names, 2) check if dialogues are between character names, and 3) check if all character names are within two scene boundaries. Using this methodology, we were able to tag 222 movies that pass the sanity check.

Data	# S	# N	# C	# D	# M
TRAIN	2,445	21,619	11,464	23,814	3,339
DEV1	714	7,495	4,431	9,378	467
DEV2	413	5,431	2,126	4,755	762
TEST	164	845	1,582	3,221	308

Table 1: Data distribution

Table 1 gives the distribution of our training, development and test sets. We use a random subset of the aforementioned set of 222 movies for training purposes, and another random subset for development. We chose 14 movies for the training set and 9 for the development set. Since human annotation for the task is expensive, instead of getting all 23 movies checked for correctness, we asked an annotator to only look at the development set (9 movies). The annotator reported that one out of 9 movies was not correctly tagged. We removed this movie from the development set. From the remaining 8 movies, we chose 5 as the first development set and the remaining 3 as the second development set. For the test set, we asked our annotator to annotate a randomly chosen screenplay (*Silver Linings Playbook*) from scratch. We chose this screenplay from the set of movies that we were unable to tag automatically, i.e. *not* from the set of 222 movies.

5 Baseline System

Gil et al. (2011) mention the use of regular expressions for tagging screenplays. However, they do not specify the regular expressions or their exact methodology. We use common knowledge about the structure of the screenplay (underlined text in section 2) to build a baseline system, that uses regular expressions and takes into account the grammar of screenplays.

Since scene descriptions, characters and dialogues are relative to the scene boundary, we do a first pass on the screenplay to tag scene boundaries. We created a dictionary of words that are expected to indicate scene boundaries. We use this dictionary for tagging lines in the screenplay with the tag "S". We tag all the lines that contain tags indicating a character (V.O., O.S.) with "C". We built a dictionary of meta-data tags that contains patterns such as "CUT TO:, DISSOLVE TO." We tag all the remaining untagged lines containing these patterns with the tag "M." This exhausts the list of regular expression matches that indicate a certain tag.

In the next pass, we incorporate prior knowledge that scene boundaries and character names are capitalized. For this, we tag all the untagged lines that are capitalized, and that have more than three words as scene boundaries (tag "S"). We tag all the untagged lines that are capitalized, and that have less than four words as character (tag "C"). The choice of the number four is not arbitrary; we examined the set of 222 screenplays that was tagged using indentation information and found that less than two percent of the character names were of length greater than three.

Finally, we incorporate prior knowledge about relative positions of dialogues and scene descriptions to tag the remaining untagged lines with one of two tags: "D" or "N". We tag all the untagged lines between a scene boundary and the first character occurrence as "N". We tag all the lines between consecutive character occurrences, the last character occurrence and the scene boundary as "D".

We use this baseline system, which incorporates all of the prior knowledge about the structure of screenplays, to tag movies in our first development set DEV1 (section 8). We report a macro-F1 measure for the five tags as 0.96. This confirms that our baseline is well suited to parse screenplays that are well structured.

6 Machine Learning Approach

Note that our baseline system is not dependent on the level of indentation (it achieves a high macro-F1 measure without using indentation information). Therefore, we have already dealt with one common problem with screenplays found on the web: bad indentation. However, there are other problems, some of which we noticed in the limited data we manually examined, and others that we anticipate: (1) missing scene boundary specific patterns (such as INT./EXT.) from the scene boundary lines, (2) uncapitalized scene boundaries and (3) uncapitalized character names. These are problems that a regular expression based system is not well equipped to deal with. In this section, we discuss a strategy for dealing with screenplays, which might have anomalies in their structure, without requiring additional annotations.

We *synthesize* training and development data to *learn* to handle the aforementioned three types of anomalies. We create eight copies of our TRAIN set: one with no anomalies, represented as TRAIN_000, [3] one in which character names are uncapitalized, represented as TRAIN_001, one in which both scene boundaries and character names are uncapitalized, represented as TRAIN_011, and so on. Similarly, we create eight copies of our DEV1 set: {DEV1_000, DEV1_001, ..., DEV1_111}. Now we have eight training and eight development sets. We train eight models, and choose the parameters for each model by tuning on the respective development set. However, at test time, we require one model. Moreover, our model should be able to handle all types of anomalies (all of which could be present in a random order). We experiment with three ensemble learning techniques and choose the one that performs the best on the second development set, DEV2. We add all three types of anomalies, randomly, to our DEV2 set.

For training individual models, we use Support Vector Machines (SVMs), and represent data as feature vectors, discussed in the next section.

[3] Each bit refers to the one type of anomaly described in the previous paragraph. If the least significant bit is 1, this means, the type of anomaly is uncapitalized characters names.

7 Features

We have six sets of features: bag-of-words features (BOW), bag-of-punctuation-marks features (BOP), bag-of-terminology features (BOT), bag-of-frames features (BOF), bag-of-parts-of-speech features (POS), and hand-crafted features (HAND).

We convert each line of a screenplay (input example) into a feature vector of length 5,497: 3,946 for BOW, 22 for BOP, 2*58 for BOT, 2*45 for POS, 2*651 for BOF, and 21 for HAND.

BOW, BOP, and BOT are binary features; we record the presence or absence of elements of each bag in the input example. The number of terminology features is multiplied by two because we have one binary vector for "contains term", and another binary vector for "is term." We have two sets of features for POS and BOF. One set is binary and similar to other binary features that record the presence or absence of parts-of-speech and frames in the input example. The other set is numeric. We record the normalized counts of each part-of-speech and frame respectively. The impetus to design this second set of features for parts-of-speech and frames is the following: we expect some classes to have a characteristic distribution of parts-of-speech and frames. For example, scene boundaries contain the location and time of scene. Therefore, we expect them to have a majority of *nouns*, and frames that are related to location and time. For the scene boundary in Figure 1 (*EXT. FBI ACADEMY ... - DAY*), we find the following distribution of parts of speech and frames: 100% nouns, 50% frame LOCALE (with frame evoking element *grounds*), and 50% frame CALENDRIC_UNIT (with frame evoking element *DAY*). Similarly, we expect the character names to have 100% nouns, and no frames.

We use Stanford part-of-speech tagger (Toutanova et al., 2003) for obtaining the part-of-speech tags and Semafor (Chen et al., 2010) for obtaining the FrameNet (Baker et al., 1998) frames present in each line of the screenplay.

We devise 21 hand-crafted features. Sixteen of these features are binary (0/1). We list these features here (the feature names are self-explanatory): has-non-alphabetical-chars, has-digits-majority, has-alpha-majority, is-quoted, capitalization (has-all-caps, is-all-caps), scene boundary (has-INT, has-EXT), date (has-date, is-date), number (has-number, is-number), and parentheses (is-parenthesized, starts-with-parenthesis, ends-with-parenthesis, contains-parenthesis). We bin the preceding number of blank lines into four bins: 0 for no preceding blank lines, 1 for one preceding blank line, 2 for two preceding blank lines, and so on. We also bin the percentage of capitalized words into four bins: 0 for the percentage of capitalized words lying between 0-25%, 1 for 25-50%, and so on. We use three numeric features: number of non-space characters (normalized by the maximum number of non-space characters in any line in a screenplay), number of words (normalized by the maximum number of words in any line in a screenplay), and number of characters (normalized by the maximum number of characters in any line in a screenplay).

For each line, say $line_i$, we incorporate context up to x lines. Figure 1 shows the lines at context -2 and +3 for the line containing the text *CRAWFORD*. To do so, we append the feature vector for $line_i$ by the feature vectors of $line_{i-1}, line_{i-2}, \ldots line_{i-x}$ and $line_{i+1}, line_{i+2}, \ldots line_{i+x}$. x is one of the parameters we tune at the time of training. We refer to this parameter as CONTEXT.

8 Experiments and Results

In this section, we present experiments and results for the task of tagging the lines of a screenplay with one of five tags: {S, N, C, D, M}. Table 1 shows the data distribution. For parameter tuning, we use DEV1 (section 8.1). We train separate models on different types of known and anticipated anomalies (as discussed in section 6). In section 8.2, we present strategies for combining these models. We select the right combination of models and features by tuning on DEV2. Finally, we show results on the test set, TEST. For all our experiments, we use the default parameters of SVM as implemented by the SMO algorithm of Weka (Hall et al., 2009). We use a linear kernel.[4]

8.1 Tuning learning parameters

We tune two parameters: the amount of training data and the amount of CONTEXT (section 7) required for learning. We do this for each of the eight models (TRAIN_000/DEV1_000, ..., TRAIN_111/DEV1_111). We merge training

[4]We tried the polynomial kernel up to a degree of four and the RBF kernel. They performed worse than the linear kernel.

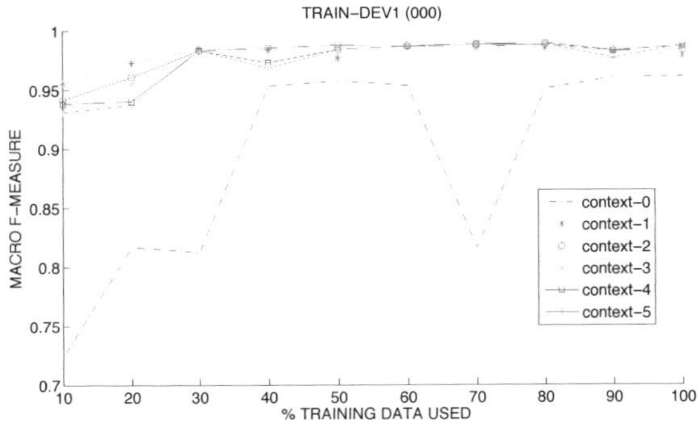

Figure 2: Learning curve for training on TRAIN_000 and testing on DEV1_000. X-axis is the % of training data, in steps of 10%. Y-axis is the macro-F1 measure for the five classes.

data from all 14 movies into one (TRAIN). We then randomize the data and split it into 10 pieces (maintaining the relative proportions of the five classes). We plot a learning curve by adding 10% of training data at each step.

Figure 2 shows the learning curve for training a model on TRAIN_000 and testing on DEV1_000.[5] The learning curve shows that the performance of our classifier without any context is significantly worse than the classifiers trained on context. Moreover, the learning saturates early, and stabilizes at about 50% of the training data. From the learning curves, we pick CONTEXT equal to 1, and the amount of training data equal to 50% of the entire training set.

Table 2 shows a comparison of our rule based baseline with the models trained using machine learning. For the 000 setting, when there is no anomaly in the screenplay, our rule based baseline performs well, achieving a macro-F1 measure of 0.96. However, our machine learning model outperforms the baseline by a statistically significant margin, achieving a macro-F1 measure of 0.99. We calculate statistical significance using McNemar's significance test, with significance defined as $p < 0.05$.[6] Results in Table 2 also show that while a deterministic regular-expression based system is not well equipped to handle anomalies, there is enough value in our feature set, that our machine learning based models learn to adapt to any combination of the three types of anomalies, achieving a high F1-measure of 0.98 on average.

[5]Learning curves for all our other models were similar.

[6]We use the same test for reporting other statistically significance results in the paper.

8.2 Finding the right ensemble and feature selection

We have trained eight separate models, which need to be combined into one model that we will make predictions at the test time. We explore the following ways of combining these models:

1. MAJ: Given a test example, we get a vote from each of our eight models, and take a majority vote. At times of a clash, we pick one randomly.

2. MAX: We pick the class predicted by the model that has the highest confidence in its prediction. Since the confidence values are real numbers, we do not see any clashes.

3. MAJ-MAX: We use MAJ but at times of a clash, we pick the class predicted by the classifier that has the highest confidence (among the classifiers that clash).

Table 3 shows macro-F1 measures for the three movies in our DEV2 set. Note, we added the three types of anomalies (section 6) randomly to the DEV2 set for tuning the type of ensemble. We compare the performance of the three ensemble techniques with the individual classifiers (trained on TRAIN_000, ... TRAIN_111).

The results show that all our ensembles (except MAX for the movie *The Last Temptation of Christ*) perform better than the individual models. Moreover, the MAJ-MAX ensemble outperforms the other two by a statistically significant margin. We thus choose MAJ-MAX as our final classifier.

Table 4 shows results for removing one of all feature sets, one at a time. These results are for our final model, MAJ-MAX. The row "All" shows the results when we use all our features for training. The consecutive rows show the result when we remove the mentioned feature set. For example, the row "- BOW" shows the result for our classifier that was trained without the bag of words feature set.

Table 4 shows that the performance drops the most for bag of words (BOW) and for our hand-crafted features (HAND). The next highest drop is for the bag of frames feature set (BOF). Error analysis revealed that the major drop in performance because of the removal of the BOF features was *not* due the drop in the performance of scene boundaries, counter to our initial intuition. The drop was because the recall of dia-

	000	001	010	011	100	101	110	111
Rule based	0.96	0.49	0.70	0.23	0.93	0.46	0.70	0.24
ML model	**0.99**	**0.99**	**0.98**	**0.99**	**0.97**	**0.98**	**0.98**	**0.98**

Table 2: Comparison of performance (macro-F1 measure) of our rule based baseline with our machine learning based models on development sets DEV1_000, DEV1_001, ..., DEV1_111. All models are trained on 50% of the training set, with the feature space including CONTEXT equal to 1.

Movie	000	001	010	011	100	101	110	111	MAJ	MAX	MAJ-MAX
LTC	0.87	0.83	0.79	0.94	0.91	0.86	0.79	0.96	0.97	0.95	**0.98**
X-files	0.87	0.84	0.79	0.93	0.86	0.84	0.79	0.92	0.94	0.94	**0.96**
Titanic	0.87	0.87	0.81	0.94	0.86	0.83	0.82	0.93	0.94	0.95	**0.97**
Average	0.87	0.85	0.80	0.94	0.88	0.84	0.80	0.94	0.95	0.95	**0.97**

Table 3: Macro-F1 measure for the five classes for testing on DEV2 set. 000 refers to the model trained on data TRAIN_000, 001 refers to the model trained on data TRAIN_001, and so on. MAJ, MAX, and MAJ-MAX are the three ensembles. The first column is the movie name. LTC refers to the movie "The Last Temptation of Christ."

Feature set	LTC	X-files	Titanic
All	0.98	0.96	0.97
- BOW	**0.94**	**0.92**	**0.94**
- BOP	0.98	**0.97**	0.97
- BOT	**0.97**	**0.95**	**0.96**
- BOF	**0.96**	**0.93**	**0.96**
- POS	0.98	0.96	**0.95**
- HAND	**0.94**	**0.93**	**0.93**

Table 4: Performance of MAJ-MAX classifier with feature removal. Statistically significant differences are in bold.

	Baseline			MAJ-MAX		
Tag	P	R	F1	P	R	F1
S	0.27	1.00	0.43	0.99	1.00	**0.99**
N	0.21	0.06	0.09	0.88	0.95	**0.91**
C	0.89	1.00	0.94	1	0.92	**0.96**
D	0.99	0.94	0.96	0.98	0.998	**0.99**
M	0.68	0.94	0.79	0.94	0.997	**0.97**
Avg	0.61	0.79	0.69	0.96	0.97	**0.96**

Table 5: Performance comparison of our rule based baseline with our best machine learning model on the five classes.

	$\mathcal{N}_B$	$\mathcal{N}_{\text{MAJ-MAX}}$	$\mathcal{N}_G$
# Nodes	202	37	41
# Links	1252	331	377
Density	0.036	0.276	0.255

Table 6: A comparison of network statistics for the three networks extracted from the movie *Silver Linings Playbook*.

logues decreases significantly. The BOF features were helping in disambiguating between the meta-data, which usually have no frames associated with them, and dialogues. Removing bag of punctuation (BOP) results in a significant increase in the performance for the movie *X-files*, with a small increase for other two movies. We remove this feature from our final classifier. Removing parts of speech (POS) results in a significant drop in the overall performance for the movie *Titanic*. Error analysis revealed that the drop in performance here was in fact due the drop in performance of scene boundaries. Scene boundaries almost always have 100% nouns and the POS features help in capturing this characteristic distribution indicative of scene boundaries. Removing bag of terminology (BOT) results in a significant drop in the overall performance of all movies. Our results also show that though the drop in performance for some feature sets is larger than the others, it is the conjunction of all features that is responsible for a high F1-measure.

8.3 Performance on the test set

Table 5 shows a comparison of the performance of our rule based baseline with our best machine learning based model on our test set, TEST. The results show that our machine learning based models outperform the baseline with a large and sig-

Model	Degree	Weighted Degree	Closeness	Betweenness	PageRank	Eigen
$\mathcal{N}_B$	0.919	0.986	0.913	0.964	0.953	0.806
$\mathcal{N}_{\text{MAJ-MAX}}$	**0.997**	**0.997**	**0.997**	**0.997**	**0.998**	**0.992**

Table 7: A comparison of Pearson's correlation coefficients of various centrality measures for $\mathcal{N}_B$ and $\mathcal{N}_{\text{MAJ-MAX}}$ with $\mathcal{N}_G$.

nificant margin on all five classes (0.96 versus 0.69 macro-F1 measure respectively). Note, as expected, the recall of the baseline is generally high, while the precision is low. Moreover, for this test set, the baseline performs relatively well on tagging character names and dialogues. However, we believe that the performance of the baseline is unpredictable. It may get *lucky* on screenplays that are well-structured (in one way or the other), but it is hard to comment on the robustness of its performance. On the contrary, our ensemble is robust, hedging its bets on eight models, which are trained to handle different types and combinations of anomalies.

In tables 6 and 7, we present an extrinsic evaluation on the test set. We extract a network from our test movie screenplay (*Silver Linings Playbook*) by using the tags of the screenplay as follows (Weng et al., 2009): we connect all characters having a dialogue with each other in a scene with links. Nodes in this network are characters, and links between two characters signal their participation in the same scene. We form three such networks: 1) based on the gold tags ($\mathcal{N}_G$), 2) based on the tags predicted by MAJ-MAX ($\mathcal{N}_{\text{MAJ-MAX}}$), and 3) based on the tags predicted by our baseline ($\mathcal{N}_B$). Table 6 compares the number of nodes, number of links, and graph density of the three networks. It is clear from the table that the network extracted by using the tags predicted by MAJ-MAX is *closer* to the gold network.

Centrality measures are one of the most fundamental social network analysis metrics used by social scientists (Wasserman and Faust, 1994). Table 7 presents a comparison of Pearson's correlation coefficient for various centrality measures for $\{\mathcal{N}_B, \mathcal{N}_G\}$, and $\{\mathcal{N}_{\text{MAJ-MAX}}, \mathcal{N}_G\}$ for the top ten characters in the movie. The table shows that across all these measures, the statistics obtained using the network $\mathcal{N}_{\text{MAJ-MAX}}$ are significantly more correlated to the gold network ($\mathcal{N}_G$), as compared the the baseline network ($\mathcal{N}_B$).

9 Conclusion and Future Work

In this paper, we presented a formalization of the task of parsing movie screenplays. We presented an NLP and ML based approach to the task, and showed that this approach outperforms the regular expression based approach by a large and significant margin. One of the main challenges we faced early on was the absence of training and test data. We proposed a methodology for learning to handle anomalies in the structure of screenplays without requiring additional annotations. We believe that the machine learning approach proposed in this paper is general, and may be used for parsing noisy documents outside of the context of movie screenplays.

In the future, we will apply our approach to parse other semi-structured sources of social networks such as television show series and theatrical plays.

Acknowledgments

We would like to thank anonymous reviewers for their useful comments. We would also like to thank Caronae Howell for her insightful comments. Agarwal was funded by IBM Ph.D. fellowship 2013-2014. This paper is based upon work supported in part by the DARPA DEFT Program. The views expressed are those of the authors and do not reflect the official policy or position of the Department of Defense or the U.S. Government.

References

Apoorv Agarwal and Owen Rambow. 2010. Automatic detection and classification of social events. In *Proceedings of the 2010 Conference on Empirical Methods in Natural Language Processing*, pages 1024–1034, Cambridge, MA, October. Association for Computational Linguistics.

Apoorv Agarwal, Anup Kotalwar, and Owen Rambow. 2013a. Automatic extraction of social networks from literary text: A case study on alice in wonderland. *In the Proceedings of the 6th International Joint Conference on Natural Language Processing (IJCNLP 2013).*

Apoorv Agarwal, Anup Kotalwar, Jiehan Zheng, and Owen Rambow. 2013b. Sinnet: Social interaction network extractor from text. In *Sixth International Joint Conference on Natural Language Processing*, page 33.

C. Baker, C. Fillmore, and J. Lowe. 1998. The berkeley framenet project. *Proceedings of the 17th international conference on Computational linguistics*, 1.

Desai Chen, Nathan Schneider, Dipanjan Das, and Noah A. Smith. 2010. Semafor: Frame argument resolution with log-linear models. In *Proceedings of the 5th International Workshop on Semantic Evaluation*, pages 264–267, Uppsala, Sweden, July. Association for Computational Linguistics.

David K. Elson, Nicholas Dames, and Kathleen R. McKeown. 2010. Extracting social networks from literary fiction. *Proceedings of the 48th Annual Meeting of the Association for Computational Linguistics*, pages 138–147.

Sebastian Gil, Laney Kuenzel, and Suen Caroline. 2011. Extraction and analysis of character interaction networks from plays and movies. Technical report, Stanford University.

Mark Hall, Eibe Frank, Geoffrey Holmes, Bernhard Pfahringer, Peter Reutemann, and Ian H. Witten. 2009. The weka data mining software: An update. *SIGKDD Explorations*, 11.

Hua He, Denilson Barbosa, and Grzegorz Kondrak. 2013. Identification of speakers in novels. *The 51st Annual Meeting of the Association for Computational Linguistics (ACL 2013).*

Kristina Toutanova, Dan Klein, Christopher Manning, and Yoram Singer. 2003. Feature-rich part-of-speech tagging with a cyclic dependency network. *In Proceedings of HLT-NAACL.*

Robert Turetsky and Nevenka Dimitrova. 2004. Screenplay alignment for closed-system speaker identification and analysis of feature films. In *Multimedia and Expo, 2004. ICME'04. 2004 IEEE International Conference on*, volume 3, pages 1659–1662. IEEE.

Stanley Wasserman and Katherine Faust. 1994. *Social Network Analysis: Methods and Applications*. New York: Cambridge University Press.

Chung-Yi Weng, Wei-Ta Chu, and Ja-Ling Wu. 2006. Movie analysis based on roles' social network. *In Proceedings of IEEE Int. Conference Multimedia and Expo.*, pages 1403–1406.

Chung-Yi Weng, Wei-Ta Chu, and Ja-Ling Wu. 2007. Rolenet: treat a movie as a small society. In *Proceedings of the international workshop on Workshop on multimedia information retrieval*, pages 51–60. ACM.

Chung-Yi Weng, Wei-Ta Chu, and Ja-Ling Wu. 2009. Rolenet: Movie analysis from the perspective of social networks. *Multimedia, IEEE Transactions on*, 11(2):256–271.

Function Words in Authorship Attribution From Black Magic to Theory?

Mike Kestemont
University of Antwerp
CLiPS Computational Linguistics Group
Prinsstraat 13, D.188
B-2000, Antwerp
Belgium
mike.kestemont@uantwerpen.be

Abstract

This position paper focuses on the use of function words in computational authorship attribution. Although recently there have been multiple successful applications of authorship attribution, the field is not particularly good at the explication of methods and theoretical issues, which might eventually compromise the acceptance of new research results in the traditional humanities community. I wish to partially help remedy this lack of explication and theory, by contributing a theoretical discussion on the use of function words in stylometry. I will concisely survey the attractiveness of function words in stylometry and relate them to the use of character n-grams. At the end of this paper, I will propose to replace the term 'function word' by the term 'functor' in stylometry, due to multiple theoretical considerations.

1 Introduction

Computational authorship attribution is a popular application in current stylometry, the computational study of writing style. While there have been significant advances recently, it has been noticed that the field is not particularly good at the explication of methods, let alone at developing a generally accepted theoretical framework (Craig, 1999; Daelemans, 2013). Much of the research in the field is dominated by an 'an engineering perspective': if a certain attribution technique performs well, many researchers do not bother to explain or interpret this from a theoretical perspective. Thus, many methods and procedures continue to function as a black box, a situation which might eventually compromise the acceptance of experimental results (e.g. new attributions) by scholars in the traditional humanities community.

In this short essay I wish to try to help partially remedy this lack of theoretical explication, by contributing a focused theoretical discussion on the use of function words in stylometry. While these features are extremely popular in present-day research, few studies explicitly address the methodological implications of using this word category. I will concisely survey the use of function words in stylometry and render more explicit why this word category is so attractive when it comes to authorship attribution. I will deliberately use a generic language that is equally intelligible to people in linguistic as well as literary studies. Due to multiple considerations, I will argue at the end of this paper that it might be better to replace the term 'function word' by the term 'functor' in stylometry.

2 Seminal Work

Until recently, scholars agreed on the supremacy of word-level features in computational authorship studies. In a 1994 overview paper Holmes (1994, p. 87) claimed that 'to date, no stylometrist has managed to establish a methodology which is better able to capture the style of a text than that based on lexical items'. Important in this respect is a line of research initiated by Mosteller and Wallace (1964), whose work marks the onset of so-called non-traditional authorship studies (Holmes, 1994; Holmes, 1998). Their work can be contrasted with the earlier philological practice of authorship attribution (Love, 2002), often characterized by a lack of a clearly defined methodological framework. Scholars adopted widely diverging attribution methodologies, the quality of whose results remained difficult to assess in the absence of a scientific consensus about a best practice (Stamatatos, 2009; Luyckx, 2010). Generally speaking, scholars' subjective intuitions (*Gelehrtenintuition*, *connoisseurship*) played far too large a role and the low level of methodological explicitness in early (e.g. nineteenth century) style-based authorship studies firmly contrasts with today's prevailing criteria for scientific research, such as replicability or transparency.

Apart from the rigorous quantification Mosteller and Wallace pursued, their work is often praised because of a specific methodological novelty they introduced: the emphasis on so-called function words. Earlier authorship attribution was often based on checklists of stylistic features, which scholars extracted from known oeuvres. Based on their previous reading experiences, expert readers tried to collect style markers that struck them as typical for an oeuvre. The attribution of works of unclear provenance would then happen through a comparison of this text's style to an author's checklist (Love, 2002, p. 185–193). The checklists were of course hand-tailored and often only covered a limited set of style markers, in which lexical features were for instance freely mixed with hardly comparable syntactic features. Because the checklist's construction was rarely documented, it seemed a matter of scholarly taste which features were included in the list, while it remained unclear why others were absent from it.

Moreover, exactly because these lists were hand-selected, they were dominated by striking stylistic features that because of their low overall frequency seemed whimsicalities to the human expert. Such low-frequency features (e.g. an uncommon noun) are problematic in authorship studies, since they are often tied to a specific genre or topic. If such a characteristic was absent in an anonymous text, it did not necessarily argue against a writer's authorship in whose other texts (perhaps in different topics or genres) the characteristic did prominently feature. Apart from the limited scalability of such style (Luyckx, 2010; Luyckx and Daelemans, 2011), a far more troublesome issue is associated with them. Because of their whimsical nature these low-frequency phenomena could have struck an author's imitators or followers as strongly as they could have struck a scholar. When trying to imitate someone's style (e.g. within the same stylistic school), those low-frequency features are the first to copy in the eyes of forgers (Love, 2002, p. 185–193). The fundamental novelty of the work by Mosteller and Wallace was that they advised to move away from a language's low-frequency features to a language's high-frequency features, which often tend to be function words.

3 Content vs Function

Let us briefly review why function words are interesting in authorship attribution. In present-day linguistics, two main categories of words are commonly distinguished (Morrow, 1986, p. 423). The open-class category includes content words, such as nouns, adjectives or verbs (Clark and Clark, 1977). This class is typically large – there are many nouns – and easy to expand – new nouns are introduced every day. The closed-class category of function words refers to a set of words (prepositions, particles, determiners) that is much smaller and far more difficult to expand – it is hard to invent a new preposition. Words from the open class can be meaningful in isolation because of their straightforward semantics (e.g. 'cat'). Function words, however, are heavily grammaticalized and often do not carry a lot of meaning in isolation (e.g. 'the'). Although the set of distinct function words is far smaller than the set of open-class words, function words are far more frequently used than content words (Zipf, 1949). Consequently, less than 0.04% of our vocabulary accounts for over half of the words we actually use in daily speech (Chung et al., 2007, p. 347). Function words have methodological advantages in the study of authorial style (Binongo, 2003, p. 11), for instance:

- All authors writing in the same language and period are bound to use the very same function words. Function words are therefore a reliable base for textual comparison;
- Their high frequency makes them interesting from a quantitative point of view, since we have many observations for them;
- The use of function words is not strongly affected by a text's topic or genre: the use of the article 'the', for instance, is unlikely to be influenced by a text's topic.
- The use of function words seems less under an author's conscious control during the writing process.

Any (dis)similarities between texts regarding function words are therefore relatively content-independent and can be far more easily associated with authorship than topic-specific stylistics. The underlying idea behind the use of function words for authorship attribution is seemingly contradictory: we look for (dis)similarities between texts that have been reduced to a number of features in which texts should not differ at all (Juola, 2006, p. 264–65).

Nevertheless, it is dangerous to blindly overestimate the degree of content-independence of function words. A number of studies have shown that function words, and especially (personal) pronouns, do correlate with genre, narrative perspective, an author's gender or even a text's topic (Herring and Paolillo, 2006; Biber et al., 2006; Newman et al., 2008). A classic reference in this respect is John Burrows's pioneering study of, amongst other topics, the use of function words in Jane Austen's novels (Burrows, 1987). This explains why many studies into authorship will in fact perform so-called 'pronoun culling' or the automated deletion of (personal) pronouns which seem too heavily connected to a text's narrative perspective or genre. Numerous empirical studies have nevertheless demonstrated that various analyses restricted to higher frequency strata, yield reliable indications about a text's authorship (Argamon and Levitan, 2005; Stamatatos, 2009; Koppel et al., 2009).

It has been noted that the switch from content words to function words in authorship attribution studies has an interesting historic parallel in art-historic research (Kestemont et al., 2012). Many paintings have survived anonymously as well, hence the large-scale research into the attribution of them. Giovanni Morelli (1816-1891) was among the first to suggest that the attribution of, for instance, a *Quattrocento* painting to some Italian master, could not happen based on 'content' (Wollheim, 1972, p. 177ff). What kind of coat Mary Magdalene was wearing or the particular depiction of Christ in a crucifixion scene seemed all too much dictated by a patron's taste, contemporary trends or stylistic influences. Morelli thought it better to restrict an authorship analysis to discrete details such as ears, hands and feet: such fairly functional elements are naturally very frequent in nearly all paintings, because they are to some extent content-independent. It is an interesting illustration of the surplus value of function words in stylometry that the study of authorial style in art history should depart from the ears, hands and feet in a painting – its inconspicuous function words, so to speak.

4 Subconsciousness

Recall the last advantage listed above: the argument is often raised that the use of these words would not be under an author's conscious control during the writing process (Stamatatos, 2009; Binongo, 2003; Argamon and Levitan, 2005; Peng et al., 2003). This would indeed help to explain why function words might act as an author invariant throughout an oeuvre (Koppel et al., 2009, p. 11). Moreover, from a methodological point of view, this would have to be true for forgers and imitators as well, hence, rendering function words resistant to stylistic imitation and forgery. Surprisingly, this claim is rarely backed up by scholarly references in the stylometric literature – an exception seems Koppel et al. (2009, p. 11) with a concise reference to Chung et al. (2007). Nevertheless, some attractive references in this respect can be found in psycholinguistic literature. Interesting is the experiment in which people have to quickly count how often the letter 'f' occurs in the following sentence:

Finished files are the result
of years of scientific study
combined with the experience
of many years.

It is common for most people to spot only four or five instances of all six occurrences of the grapheme (Schindler, 1978). Readers commonly miss the *f*s in the preposition 'of' in the sentence. This is consistent with other reading research showing that readers have more difficulties in spotting spelling errors in function words than in content words (Drewnowski and Healy, 1977). A similar effect is associated with phrases like 'Paris in the the spring' (Aronoff and Fudeman, 2005, p. 40–41). Experiments have demonstrated that during their initial reading, many people will not be aware of the duplication of the article 'the'. Readers typically fail to spot such errors because they take the use of function words for granted – note that this effect would be absent for 'Paris in the spring spring', in which a content word is wrongly duplicated. Such a subconscious attitude needs not imply that function words would be unimportant in written communication. Consider the following passage:[1]

> Aoccdrnig to a rscheearch at Cmabrigde Uinervtisy, it deosn't mttaer in waht oredr the ltteers in a wrod are, the olny iprmoetnt tihng is taht the frist and lsat ltteer be at the rghit pclae. The rset can be a toatl mses and you can sitll raed it wouthit porbelm. Tihs is bcuseae the huamn mnid deos not raed ervey lteter by istlef, but the wrod as a wlohe.

Although the words' letters in this passage seem randomly jumbled, the text is still relatively readable (Rawlinson, 1976). As the quote playfully states itself, it is vital in this respect that the first and final letter of each word are not moved – and, depending on the language, this is in fact not the only rule that must be obeyed. It is crucial however that this limitation causes the shorter function words in running English text to remain fairly intact (McCusker et al., 1981). The intact nature alone of the function words in such jumbled text, in fact greatly adds to the readability of such passages. Thus, while function words are vital to structure linguistic information in our communication (Morrow, 1986), psycholinguistic research suggests that they do not attract attention to themselves in the same way as content words do.

Unfortunately, it should be stressed that all references discussed in this section are limited to reader's experience, and not writer's experience. While there will exist similarities between a language user's perception and production of function words, it cannot be ruled out that writers will take on a much more conscious attitude towards function words than readers. Nevertheless, the apparent inattentiveness with which readers approach function words might be reminiscent of a writer's attitude towards them, although much more research would be needed in order to properly substantiate this hypothesis.

5 Character N-grams

Recall Holmes's 1994 claim that 'to date, no stylometrist has managed to establish a methodology which is better able to capture the style of a text than that based on lexical items' (Holmes, 1994, p. 87). In 1994 other types of style markers (e.g. syntactical) were – in isolation – never able to outperform lexical style markers (Van Halteren et al., 2005). Interestingly, advanced feature selection methods did not always outperform frequency-based selection methods, that plainly singled out function words (Argamon and Levitan, 2005; Stamatatos, 2009). The supremacy of function words was challenged, however, later in the 1990s when character n-grams came to the fore (Kjell, 1994). This representation was originally borrowed from the field of Information Retrieval where the technique had been used in automatic language identification. Instead of cutting texts up into words, this particular text representation segmented a text into a series of consecutive, partially overlapping groups of n characters. A first order n-gram model only considers so-called unigrams ($n = 1$); a second order n-gram model considers bigrams ($n = 2$), and so forth. Note that word boundaries are typically explicitly represented: for instance, ' b', 'bi', 'ig', 'gr', 'ra', 'am', 'm '.

Since Kjell (1994), character n-grams have proven to be the best performing feature type in state-of-the-art authorship attribution (Juola, 2006), although at first sight, they might seem uninformative and meaningless. Follow-up research learned that this outstanding performance was not only largely language independent but also fairly independent of the attribution algorithms used (Peng et al., 2003; Stamatatos, 2009; Koppel et al., 2009). The study of character n-grams for authorship attribution has since then significantly grown in popularity, however, mostly in the more technical literature where the technique originated. In these studies, performance issues play an important role, with researchers focusing on actual attribution accuracy in large corpora (Luyckx, 2010). This focus might help explain why, so far, few convincing attempts have been made to interpret the discriminatory qualities of characters n-grams, which is why their use (like function words) in stylometry can be likened to a sort of black magic. One explanation so far has been that these units tend to capture 'a bit of everything', being sensitive to both the content and form of a text (Houvardas and Stamatatos, 2006; Koppel et al., 2009; Stamatatos, 2009). One could wonder, however, whether such an answer does much more than reproducing the initial question:

[1]Matt Davis maintains an interesting website on this topic: `http://www.mrc-cbu.cam.ac.uk/people/matt.davis/Cmabrigde/`. I thank Bram Vandekerckhove for pointing out this website. The 'Cmabridge'-passage as well the 'of'-example have anonymously circulated on the Internet for quite a while.

Then why does it work? Moreover, Koppel et al. expressed words of caution regarding the caveats of character n-grams, since many of them 'will be closely associated to particular content words and roots' (Koppel et al., 2009, p. 13).

The reasons for this outstanding performance could partially be of a prosaic, information-theoretical nature, relating to the unit of stylistic measurement. Recall that function words are quantitatively interesting, at least partially because they are simply frequent in text. The more observations we have available per text, the more trustworthily one can represent it. Character n-grams push this idea even further, simply because texts by definition have more data points for character n-grams than for entire words (Stamatatos, 2009; Daelemans, 2013). Thus the mere number of observations, relatively larger for character n-grams than for function words, might account for their superiority from a purely quantitative perspective.

Nevertheless, more might be said on the topic. Rybicki & Eder (2011) report on a detailed comparative study of a well-known attribution technique, Burrows's Delta. John Burrows is considered one of the godfathers of modern stylometry – D.I. Holmes (1994) ranked him alongside the pioneers Mosteller and Wallace. He introduced his influential Delta-technique in his famous Busa lecture (Burrows, 2002). Many subsequent discussions agree that Delta essentially is a fairly intuitive algorithm which generally achieves decent performance (Argamon, 2008), comparing texts on the basis of the frequencies of common function words. In their introductory review of Delta's applications, Rybicki and Eder tackled the assumption of Delta's language independence: following the work of Juola (2006, p. 269), they question the assumption 'that the use of methods relying on the most frequent words in a corpus should work just as well in other languages as it does in English' (Rybicki and Eder, 2011, p. 315).

Their paper proves this assumption wrong, reporting on various, carefully set-up experiments with a corpus, comprising 7 languages (English, Polish, French, Latin, German, Hungarian and Italian). Although they consider other parameters (such as genre), their most interesting results concern language (Rybicki and Eder, 2011, p. 319–320):

> while Delta is still the most successful method of authorship attribution based on word frequencies, its success is not independent of the language of the texts studied. This has not been noticed so far for the simple reason that Delta studies have been done, in a great majority, on English-language prose. [...] The relatively poorer results for Latin and Polish, both highly inflected in comparison with English and German, suggests the degree of inflection as a possible factor. This would make sense in that the top strata of word frequency lists for languages with low inflection contain more uniform words, especially function words; as a result, the most frequent words in languages such as English are relatively more frequent than the most frequent words in agglutinative languages such as Latin.

Their point of criticism is obvious but vital: the restriction to function words for stylometric research seems sub-optimal for languages that make less use of function words. They suggest that this relatively recent discovery might be related to the fact that most of the seminal and influential work in authorship attribution has been carried out on English-language texts.

English is a typical example of a language that does not make extensive use of case endings or other forms of inflection (Sapir, 1921, chapter VI). Such weakly inflected languages express a lot of their functional linguistic information through the use of small function words, such as prepositions (e.g. 'with a sword'). Structural information in these languages tends to be expressed through minimal units of meaning or grammatical morphemes, which are typically realized as individual words (Morrow, 1986). At this point, it makes sense to contrast English with another major historical lingua franca but one that has received far less stylometric attention: Latin.

Latin is a school book example of a heavily inflected language, like Polish, that makes far more extensive use of affixes: endings that which are added to words to mark their grammatical function in a sentence. An example: in the Latin word *ensi* (ablative singular: 'with a sword') the case ending (–i) is a separate morpheme that takes on grammatical role which is similar to that of the English preposition 'with'. Nevertheless, it is not realized as a separate word separated by whitespace from surrounding morphemes. It is rather concatenated to another morpheme (ens-) expressing a more tangible meaning.

This situation renders a straightforward application of the Delta-method – so heavily biased towards words – problematic for more synthetic or agglutinative languages. What has been said about function words in previous stylometric research, obviously relates to their special status as functional linguistic items. The inter-related characteristics of 'high frequency', 'content-independence' and 'good dispersion' (Kestemont et al., 2012) even only apply to them, insofar as they are grammatical morphemes. Luckily for English, a lot of grammatical morphemes can easily be detected by splitting running text into units that do not contain whitespace or punctuation and selecting the most frequent items among them (Burrows, 2002; Stamatatos, 2009). For languages that display another linguistic logic, however, the situation is far more complicated, because the functional information contained in grammatical morphemes is more difficult to gain access to, since these need not be solely or even primarily realized as separate words. If one restricts analyses to high-frequency words in these languages, one obviously ignores a lot of the functional information inside less frequent words (e.g. inflection).

6 Functors

At the risk of being accused of quibbling about terms, I wish to argue that the common emphasis on function words in stylometry should be replaced by an emphasis on the broader concept of functors, a term which can be borrowed from psycholinguistics, used to denote grammatical morphemes (Kwon, 2005, p. 1–2) or:

> forms that do not, in any simple way, make reference. They mark grammatical structures and carry subtle modulatory meanings. The word classes or parts of speech involved (inflections, auxiliary verbs, articles, prepositions, and conjunctions) all have few members and do not readily admit new members (Brown, 1973, p. 75).

In my opinion, the introduction of the term 'functor' would have a number of advantages – the first and least important of which is that it is aesthetically more pleasing than the identical term 'grammatical morphemes'. Note, first of all, that function words – grammatical morphemes realized as individual words – are included in the definition of a functor. The concept of a functor as such does not replace the interest in function words but rather broadens it and extends it towards all grammatical morphemes, whether they be realized as individual words or not. Note how all advantages, previously only associated with function words in stylometry (high frequency, good dispersion, content-independence, unconscious use) apply to every member in the category of functors.

A second advantage has to do with language independence. Note that stylometry's ultimate goal regarding authorship seems of a universal nature: a majority of stylometrists in the end are concerned with the notorious Stylome-hypothesis (Van Halteren et al., 2005) or finding a way to characterize an author's individual writing style, regardless of text variety, time and, especially, language. Restricting the extraction of functional information from text to the word level might work for English, but seems too language-specific a methodology to be operable in many other languages, as suggested by Rybicki and Eder (2011) and earlier Juola (2006, p. 269). Stylometric research into high-frequency, functional linguistic items should therefore break up words and harvest more and better information from text. The scope of stylistic focus should be broadened to include all functors.

The superior performance of character n-grams in capturing authorial style – in English, as well as other languages – seems relevant in this respect. First of all, the most frequent n-grams in a corpus often tend to be function words: 'me', 'or' and 'to' are very frequent function words in English, but they are also very frequent character bigrams. Researchers often restrict their text representation to the most frequent n-grams in a corpus (2009, p. 541), so that n-gram approaches include function words rather than exclude them. In addition, high-frequency n-grams are often able to capture more refined grammatical information. Note how a text representation in terms of n-grams subtly exploits the presence of whitespace. In most papers advocating the use of n-grams, whitespace is explicitly encoded. Again, this allows more observations-per-word but, in addition, makes a representation sensitive to e.g. inflectional information. A high frequency of the bigram 'ed' could reflect any use of the character series (reduce vs. talked). A trigram representation 'ed ' reveals a word-final position of the character series, thus indicating it being used for expressing grammatical information through affixation. Psycholinguistic research also stresses the important status of the first letter(s) of words, especially with respect to how words are cognitively accessed in the lexicon (Rubin, 1995, p. 74). Note that this word-initial aspect too is captured under an n-gram representation (' aspect').

A widely accepted theoretical ground for the outstanding performance of character n-grams, will have to consider the fact that n-grams offer a more powerful way of capturing the functional information in text. They are sensitive to the internal morphemic structure of words, capturing many functors which are simply ignored in word-level approaches. Although some n-grams can indeed be 'closely associated to particular content words and roots' (Koppel et al., 2009, p. 13), I would be inclined to hypothesize that high-frequency n-grams work in spite of this, not because of this. This might suggest that extending techniques, like Delta, to all functors in text, instead of just function words, will increase both their performance and language independence.

A final advantage of the introduction of the concept of a functor is that it would facilitate the teaming up with a neighbouring field of research that seems extremely relevant for the field of stylometry from a theoretical perspective, but so far has only received limited attention in it: psycholinguistics. The many parallels with the reading research discussed above indicate that both fields might have a lot to learn from each other. An illustrative example is the study of functor acquisition by children. It has been suggested that similar functors are not only present in all languages of the world, but acquired by all children in an extremely similar 'natural order' (Kwon, 2005). This is intriguing given stylometry's interest in the Stylome-hypothesis. If stylometry is ultimately looking for linguistic variables that are present in each individual's *parole*, the universal aspects of functors further stress the benefits of the term's introduction. All of this justifies the question whether the functor should not become a privileged area of study in future stylometric research.

Acknowledgments

The author was funded as a postdoctoral research fellow by the Research Foundation of Flanders (FWO). The author would like to thank Matthew Munson, Bram Vandekerckhove, Dominiek Sandra, Stan Szpakowicz as well as the anonymous reviewers of this paper for their substantial feedback on earlier drafts. Finally, I am especially indebted to Walter Daelemans for the inspiring discussions on the topic of this paper.

References

S. Argamon and S. Levitan. 2005. Measuring the usefulness of function words for authorship attribution. In *Proceedings of the Joint Conference of the Association for Computers and the Humanities and the Association for Literary and Linguistic Computing (2005)*. Association for Computing and the Humanities.

S. Argamon. 2008. Interpreting Burrows's Delta: Geometric and Probabilistic Foundations. *Literary and Linguistic Computing*, (23):131–147.

M. Aronoff and K. Fudeman. 2005. *What is Morphology?* Blackwell.

D. Biber, S. Conrad, and R. Reppen. 2006. *Corpus linguistics - Investigating language structure and use.* Cambridge University Press, 5 edition.

J. Binongo. 2003. Who Wrote the 15th Book of Oz? An application of multivariate analysis to authorship attribution. *Chance*, (16):9–17.

R. Brown. 1973. *A First Language*. Harvard University Press.

J. Burrows. 1987. *Computation into Criticism: A Study of Jane Austen's Novels and an Experiment in Method.* Clarendon Press; Oxford University Press.

J. Burrows. 2002. 'Delta': a measure of stylistic difference and a guide to likely authorship. *Literary and Linguistic Computing*, (17):267–287.

C. Chung and J. Pennebaker. 2007. The psychological functions of function words. In K. Fiedler et al., editor, *Social Communication*, pages 343–359. Psychology Press.

H. Clark and E. Clark. 1977. *Psychology and language: an introduction to psycholinguistics.* Harcourt, Brace & Jovanovich.

H. Craig. 1999. Authorial attribution and computational stylistics: if you can tell authors apart, have you learned anything about them? *Literary and Linguistic Computing*, 14(1):103–113.

W. Daelemans. 2013. Explanation in Computational Stylometry. In *Proceedings of the 14th International Conference on Computational Linguistics and Intelligent Text Processing - Volume 2*, CICLing'13, pages 451–462, Berlin, Heidelberg. Springer-Verlag.

A. Drewnowski and A. Healy. 1977. Detection errors on the and and: Evidence for reading units larger than the word. *Memory & Cognition*, (5).

S. Herring and John C. Paolillo. 2006. Gender and genre variation in weblogs. *Journal of Sociolinguistics*, 10(4):439–459.

D. Holmes. 1994. Authorship Attribution. *Computers and the Humanities*, 28(2):87–106.

D. Holmes. 1998. The Evolution of Stylometry in Humanities Scholarship. *Literary and Linguistic Computing*, 13(3):111–117.

J. Houvardas and E. Stamatatos. 2006. N-gram feature selection for authorship identification. In J. Euzenat and J. Domingue, editors, *Proceedings of Artificial Intelligence: Methodologies, Systems, and Applications (AIMSA 2006)*, pages 77–86. Springer-Verlag.

P. Juola. 2006. Authorship Attribution. *Foundations and Trends in Information Retrieval*, 1(3):233–334.

M. Kestemont, W. Daelemans, and D. Sandra. 2012. Robust Rhymes? The Stability of Authorial Style in Medieval Narratives. *Journal of Quantitative Linguistics*, 19(1):1–23.

B. Kjell. 1994. Discrimination of authorship using visualization. *Information Processing and Management*, 30(1):141–50.

M. Koppel, J. Schler, and S. Argamon. 2009. Computational Methods in Authorship Attribution. *Journal of the American Society for Information Science and Technology*, 60(1):9–26.

E. Kwon. 2005. The Natural Order of Morpheme Acquisition: A Historical Survey and Discussion of Three Putative Determinants. *Teachers' College Columbia Working Papers in TESOL and Applied Linguistics*, 5(1):1–21.

H. Love. 2002. *Authorship Attribution: An Introduction*. Cambridge University Press.

K. Luyckx and W. Daelemans. 2011. The effect of author set size and data size in authorship attribution. *Literary and Linguistic Computing*, (26):35–55.

K. Luyckx. 2010. *Scalability Issues in Authorship Attribution*. Ph.D. thesis, University of Antwerp.

L. McCusker, P. Gough, and R. Bias. 1981. Word recognition inside out and outside in. *Journal of Experimental Psychology: Human Perception and Performance*, 7(3):538–551.

D. Morrow. 1986. Grammatical morphemes and conceptual structure in discourse processing. *Cognitive Science*, 10(4):423–455.

F. Mosteller and D. Wallace. 1964. *Inference and disputed authorship: The Federalist*. Addison-Wesley.

M. Newman, C. Groom, L. Handelman, and J. Pennebaker. 2008. Gender Differences in Language Use: An Analysis of 14,000 Text Samples. *Discourse Processes*, 45(3):211–236, May.

F. Peng, D. Schuurmans, V. Keselj, and S. Wang. 2003. Language independent authorship attribution using character level language models. In *Proceedings of the 10th Conference of the European Chapter of the Association for Computational Linguistics*, pages 267–274.

D. Rubin. 1995. *Memory in Oral Traditions. The Cognitive Psychology of Epic, Ballads and Counting-out Rhymes*. Oxford University Press.

J. Rybicki and M. Eder. 2011. Deeper Delta across genres and languages: do we really need the most frequent words? *Literary and Linguistic Computing*, pages 315–321.

E. Sapir. 1921. *Language: An Introduction to the Study of Speech*. Harcourt, Brace & Co.

R. Schindler. 1978. The effect of prose context on visual search for letters. *Memory & Cognition*, (6):124–130.

E. Stamatatos. 2009. A survey of modern authorship attribution methods. *Journal of the American Society For Information Science and Technology*, (60):538–556.

H. Van Halteren, H. Baayen, F. Tweedie, M. Haverkort, and A. Neijt. 2005. New Machine Learning Methods Demonstrate the Existence of a Human Stylome. *Journal of Quantitative Linguistics*, (12):65–77.

R. Wollheim. 1972. *On Art and the Mind: Essays and Lectures*. Harvard University Press.

G. Zipf. 1949. *Human Behavior and the Principle of Least Effort*. Addison-Wesley.

Author Index